I0199502

TEACHING KIDS TO
MANAGE ANXIETY

Superstar Practical Strategies

Deb Hopper

www.lifeskills4kids.com.au

Teaching Kids to Manage Anxiety: Superstar Practical Strategies.

First Published in 2019 by Deb Hopper
Life Skills 4 Kids
PO Box 210 Forster NSW 2428

©2019 Deb Hopper/ Debbie Hopper
The moral rights of the author have been asserted.

National Library of Australia Cataloguing-in-Publication entry:
Creator: Hopper, Deb, author.
Teaching Kids to Manage Anxiety: Superstar Practical Strategies
ISBN: 978-0-9944483-6-1 (hardback)
ISBN: 978-0-9944483-4-7 (paperback)
ISBN: 978-0-9944483-5-4 (e-book)

Subjects: Child psychology.
Anxiety in children.
Self-control in children.
Self-management (Psychology) for children.

Editor: Heather Hackett
Cover and internal design by Nélia Olival
Book production by Life Skills 4 Kids
Printing in Australia by Ingram Spark

DISCLAIMER

The material in this publication is of the nature of general comment only and does not represent professional advice. It is not intended to provide specific guidance for particular circumstances and it should not be relied on as the basis for any decision to take action or not take action on any matter which it covers. Readers should obtain professional advice where appropriate, before making any such decision. To the maximum extent permitted by law, the author and publisher disclaim all responsibility and liability to any person, arising directly or indirectly from any person taking or not taking action based on the information in this publication. If advice concerning health or educational care is needed, the services of a qualified professional should be sought. You should be aware of any laws that govern any education or health practices in your state.

The examples within this book are not intended to represent or guarantee that everyone or anyone will achieve their desired results. Each individual's success will be determined by their individual differences.

First edition, 2019 I Copyright 2019 by Deb Hopper
All rights reserved. No part of this book may be reproduced, stored in a retrieval system or transmitted in any form by an electronic, mechanical, photocopying, recording means or otherwise without prior written permission of the publisher.

A catalogue record for this book is available from the National Library of Australia

DEDICATION

To my boys, who have taught me many things about self-regulation and anxiety and who continue to teach me every day!

ACKNOWLEDGEMENTS

This book is the result of over 21 years of learning from hundreds of children and adults. I have loved every minute working with you all, and every child or adult I work with teaches me more about this very important topic.

Thank you, God, for your inspiration, wisdom and protection.

A big thank you to my Life Skills 4 Kids Team. You inspire me, support me, keep me going. You help forward the vision not just for our local clinic clients, but for helping children around the world. Thank you for everything.

Thank you for purchasing this book. We are very excited to include our bonus webinar where Deb explains the extent of anxiety in our children.

Access free online training today!

Scan this QR code in
or type in **http://qrs.ly/ui7bb5f**

Contents

Contents

Contents

"Through this wonderful book I was able to recognise that we often try to rescue our children from their stress and anxiety when we should actually take the opportunity to create teachable moments of how to self-regulate."

Peta C, Mum, Disabilities and Mental Health Worker

"If you are a teacher, children's counsellor or parent, then this is a must read. Deb very helpfully and clearly identifies many causes of stress and anxiety for kids. But more than that, she carefully outlines different techniques and strategies to help kids lead more regulated lives."

Peter Flower, Counsellor

"Deb Hopper brings some wonderful practical strategies to help anxious children, drawing on her many years of clinical experience as an Occupational Therapist. The Just Right Kids® Model contextualises where kids function best. A great read for all parents seeking practical help for their anxious child."

Dr Andrew Pennington, Integrative GP B.Sc. (Hons); B.Med.; DRANZCOG Adv; FRACGP; FARGP

Foreword

Deb has again produced an easy to read book that is chock full of strategies and tools for helping the children in your life. This time she addresses recognizing and helping children deal with stress and anxiety. Anxiety disorders are seen worldwide, are on the rise, and are seen in an alarming number of children. Because of these facts this common sense approach to understanding the behaviours, considering the root of the behaviours, and helping children deal with anxieties is a great resource for parents. Deb begins by presenting simple models of the brain to help us understand what may be going awry when children become so stressed or anxious that they cannot come up with strategies that help them cope. She returns to her model of brain function throughout the book, linking us back to a way of understanding behaviours and strategies. Deb defines key behaviours, words, and phrases that may indicate your child is not managing their stress very effectively and in doing so gives us a way to re-think about and reframe the child's behaviours and the language he or she uses. This approach then allows us to step back from responding to anxious statements like "Do I have to go? My stomach hurts!" with our own dismissals of "Oh, you are fine. You will feel better when you get there."

Deb introduces the construct of 'occupational anxiety'. While I don't think we need yet another new phrase in the occupational therapy literature, I appreciate the fact that within this term Deb makes a case for distinguishing the anxiety borne from engaging in daily childhood occupations from stress and anxiety that have broader causes. Through the book Deb defines 5 subtypes of occupational anxiety, walks us through identifying them and provides us with strategies and tools for addressing children's stress and anxiety.

This book addresses some of the basics of what might be called 'mindful parenting.' Deb takes on the issue of screen time and presents the procs and cons of screen time, a prickly issue for many of us. Beyond presenting the issues and some of the science behind limiting screen time for our children, Deb offers strategies and excellent reasons for why screen time should be held in check. Importantly, she talks to us, as parents ourselves, about the examples we set and some strategies we can use to reduce our own screen time.

Foreword

Revisiting the Just Right Kids® model Deb has developed and refined over several years, we now see how it is linked to stress and anxiety and how it can be used as a tool for addressing both. Deb discusses why a little stress is useful, even needed, for optimal performance, and walks us through her model of helping the child understand what is going on when their body and mind are not in the optimal zone for performance.

In the second section we are presented with a myriad of ways we can help children reduce their stress, and work through stressful and anxiety provoking events. Deb digs into the occupational therapy tool box and clearly presents the basics of how to 'construct' a morning routine that sets the child up to manage their day. And she also presents the strengths of task analysis in helping children manage their learning process, something we called 'breaking it into sound bytes' when my own children were young. This section of the book is rich with simple yet strong tools for helping yourself and your child manage stress and anxiety. Deb presents both top down and bottom up strategies, merging body and mind in preparing for the day and addressing stressful events as they emerge. And, it is not simply a cookbook of 'things to do'. The text is rich with the rationale and science behind the tools and strategies.

Stress and anxiety are ever-present in today's world. This book is a 'must read' for parents invested in understanding the issues and providing themselves and their children strategies and tools to deal with daily stresses.

Dr Shelly Lane

Introduction

Our children are growing up in a fast-paced world where information and opportunity overload can become overwhelming. The impact of this fast pace on parents and teachers pushes us all into a frantic lifestyle which can be difficult to manage.

It has been reported that 1 in 5 children in America suffer from stress[1]; this is similar to the incidence of mental health issues in adults. And 1 in 3 children report physical symptoms of stress.

The word 'stressed' is used in a general way. A child who is misbehaving, or tense, or tearful, may be said to be stressed. But when we look more closely at the situations in which we describe a child in this way, we usually find that what we are seeing is a child who is overwhelmed, one who is having difficulty managing their emotional responses to their environment, including the expectations they feel they have to live up to.

The difference between children who are able to manage their emotions and those who struggle with them, is that those who manage are able to be self-aware, to understand when they are slipping from being OK towards feeling overwhelmed or out of control. Once children are self-aware, they can be taught strategies to self-regulate and make appropriate emotional changes, and thus be more in control of their emotions and their reactions to stressful events.

Let me ask you this – does your child begin most days feeling calm, confident and ready to learn? Are they able to communicate with you at times when they are feeling overwhelmed? Does your child feel nurtured and loved in a way that they truly know and understand?

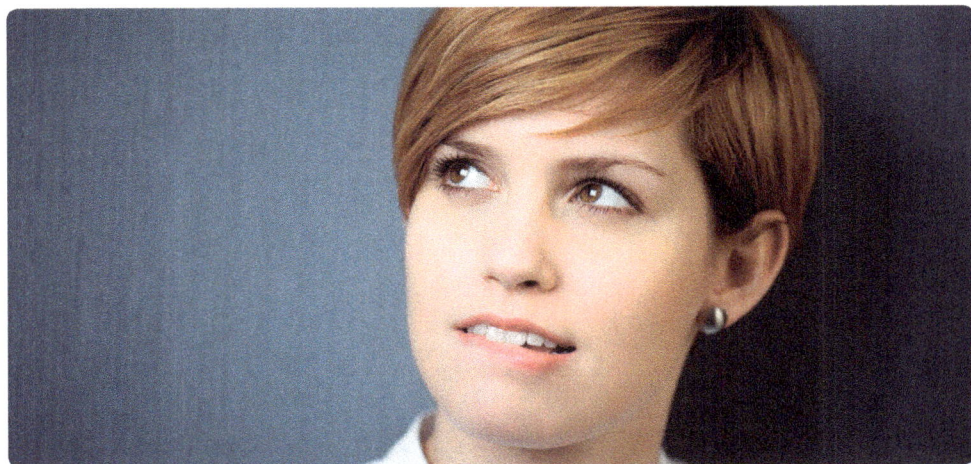

My aim in writing this book is that, once you and your child have mastered the technique it illustrates, you will be able to answer 'yes' to those questions. The book will clearly show you how, by using the *Just Right Kids® Model*, we can teach children how to identify their body's 'speed', and to identify the emotions and body responses that signal stress, including:

1. How to tune in to their body and understand what sensory issues might be contributing to their stress levels, and
2. Practical strategies for reducing stress that they can use daily to improve self-regulation and cope better with emotional difficulties.

As an Occupational Therapist working in both Paediatrics and Mental Health arenas for the past 21 years, I am fascinated by the simple strategies that can make a massive difference to a child's ability to cope. Occupational Therapists have a broad range of training, which gives us an overall view of the range of reasons which might trigger a child's difficulty in coping with emotions. It also gives us a very practical framework for working through issues of behaviour and emotional difficulties with children, using a play-based 'on the floor' approach.

Throughout this book I will be using the word '*stressed*' as an 'umbrella' term to describe children whom we might simply call 'stressed', but who may in fact be struggling with emotional or sensory overload, worry and anxiety.

This book is guided by my top 5 tips for empowering and supporting children who experience stress anxiety, worry or sensory overload, whatever the reason for the cause.

The Top 5 tips to help kids with anxiety include:

1. Understand a stressed and anxious child's body cues
   a. Fight and flight response
   b. Teach the child to understand how they feel
   c. Teach the child to label and tell you how they feel

2. Support their nervous system
   a. Muscle/ proprioception (jumping on trampoline, wall push ups)
   b. Deep touch pressure (massage, pizza game, rough and tumble play)

3. Create a mental space
   a. Stop, think, breathe

4. Get a plan together
    a. Brainstorm with kids
    b. Create a checklist – e.g. know how to go and talk to a friend, what to do, what to say
    c. Use visuals to help communicate the plan.
5. Seek professional help

Thank you for joining me on this journey to help me support your child in your corner of the world! Enjoy, and be inspired with some new ideas and resources to help your child or the children with whom you live or work.

Deb Hopper

Scan this QR code in
or type in **http://qrs.ly/ui7bb5f**

---

[1] http://www.apa.org/monitor/2011/01/stressed-america.aspx (American Psychological Association. *Stressed in America*. 2011, Vol 42, No. 1 Print version: page 60.)

CHAPTER 01

What is Stress in Children? What Does it Boil Down to?

Let's start with the basics. Stress is a common reaction when perceived expectations or demands exceed our perceived capacity to deal with them. How much stress we can handle varies from person to person. Some children are more sensitive overall, while some are more sensitive to specific stress triggers.

In this book, we will be digging deeper and looking at why children might have symptoms of stress or anxiety from some different viewpoints. Often stress or behavioural difficulties are misdiagnosed; a label may be given to a child without peeling back the layers to look at the underlying reason **why** they may be struggling.

'Stressed', as I have already mentioned, may be described as an 'umbrella' term to describe children whose emotions often overwhelm them from sensory overload, worry or anxiety. The reasons why children are overwhelmed are varied, and in this book, I will be outlining the *Just Right Kids® Model* and strategies for increasing a child's capacity to recognise when their emotions are changing, and to develop better control over them. (More information on this model is given below.) Another term for these skills is **self-regulation** – being in control of your emotions, your levels of engagement and concentration.

Having awareness, being able to label our energy levels and our emotions, and becoming engaged with what we are doing are simple concepts, but very powerful ones. Once a child develops these abilities, the door is open for them to be more independent, emotionally secure and resilient.

So, in a nutshell, if we can teach children to be emotionally aware and identify when their emotions and levels of alertness are changing, we can build on these emotional foundations and develop higher-level skills for monitoring and consciously changing their emotions. We need to teach children strategies to engage, listen and concentrate in class in early primary/elementary school before they can extend these skills to self-monitor and manage their concentration and stress levels for studying in high school and college/university.

66 Having awareness, being able to label our emotions and becoming engaged with what we are doing, are simple concepts, but very powerful ones. 99

There are two related and interconnecting concepts that we need to teach children as the foundations of emotional control, self-regulation and stress management. The first concept is 'body speed'. Body speed can be described as our level of 'busy-ness', and is often described as hyperactivity, or going 'too fast'. On the other hand, many children are under-alert. They may appear tired, lethargic and just can't get going or cue into learning. Their body is in the 'slow' zone. This is really important because so many children don't have sufficient understanding of it or are not confident enough to be able to communicate and label how they are feeling through words like 'My body or brain feels like it is running too fast.' Or, 'I don't understand what it feels like in my body when I am relaxed and chilled out'. The first part of the *Just Right Kids® Model* describes the concept of body speed. This is the 'busy-ness' side of the model.

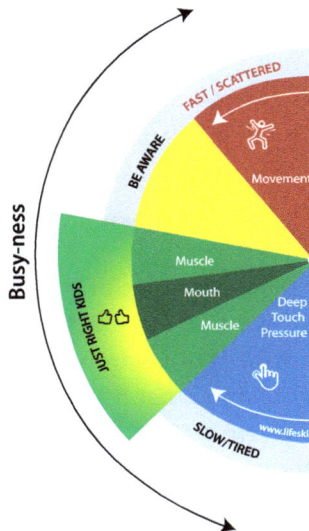

Just imagine 7-year-old Jack, who finds it difficult to sit in class to listen. His body needs to move a lot. There are many reasons why he might find it difficult to sit still, including low muscle tone, flexible joints, seeking out movement (vestibular sense). Vestibular is our 'sense of movement', which is registered in the inner ear. Many children seek out lots of movement, which feeds their nervous system, making it easier for them to listen and learn. Jack also needs to gain extra kinaesthetic/proprioception feedback to know where his body is in space in order to be organised. Proprioception is our 'kinaesthetic or internal muscle sense'. It gives us information about how to move, or how tightly to hold objects. He is noticed by his teacher as he needs to move, and he is up and down and walking around the classroom a lot. Jack's body and his brain are going fast. Jack doesn't understand this. This is how he feels all day, every day. His body and perhaps his thoughts might be described as being 'fast' or 'scattered'.

Then, we have 10-year-old Joe, whose body tends to be in the 'slow' or 'tired' zone most of the day. He just can't seem to get up and going. He tends to sit at his desk with his chin resting on his hand. Sometimes Joe is labelled as 'lazy'. He is very chilled out. He doesn't feel lazy, and it makes him sad when he hears adults or children call him this. He just finds it hard to get going, and he finds it difficult to cue in to listen at school; his thoughts tend to 'drift off'.

However, Kate, who is 8, is doing really well at school. She is able to concentrate well when she is sitting in class. She is able to sit up and listen easily and comprehend instructions from her teacher. She copes well with changes in routine, enjoys a fun, active play at lunch time and is able to transition well after lunch to further learning and listening tasks. Kate is easily able to label when she is feeling busy or tired. Most of the time, Kate has what can be called good emotional awareness and self-regulation skills.

> "I love how you give examples of three different children, two that have different dysregulation or emotional unawareness. Then you're actually saying what it looks like for a child who does have self-regulation which is good because we often get told what the negative looks like and not how it exactly should look like or feel like for the child."
>
> Peta, Mum

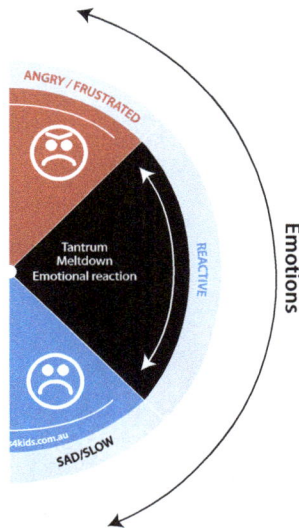

The second really important aspect of self-regulation and stress management is understanding our emotions and being able to label them accurately. This is an important foundation for developing emotional intelligence and resilience. Children need to be able to understand the difference between what it feels like to be angry or frustrated, what it feels like if they are moving towards a meltdown or tantrum, and what it feels like to be sad or low in mood. This can be shown graphically on the right-hand segment of the *Just Right Kids® Model*.

The brilliant news is that children can learn and be aware of mastering the two aspects of this technique, understanding self-regulation and emotional regulation, which stands them in good stead for handling the bigger issue of stress management now, and as they move towards adulthood.

By combining these two very different, yet connected concepts, we can see the full *Just Right Kids® Model* come together. Below, you can see the two halves of the *Just Right Kids® Model* brought together into a full circle model.

By teaching children these concepts individually and then putting them together in a fun and play-based way, we can teach them valuable life skills to increase their resilience, decrease stress and manage appropriate emotional responses both now and in the future. This book will help you do exactly that.

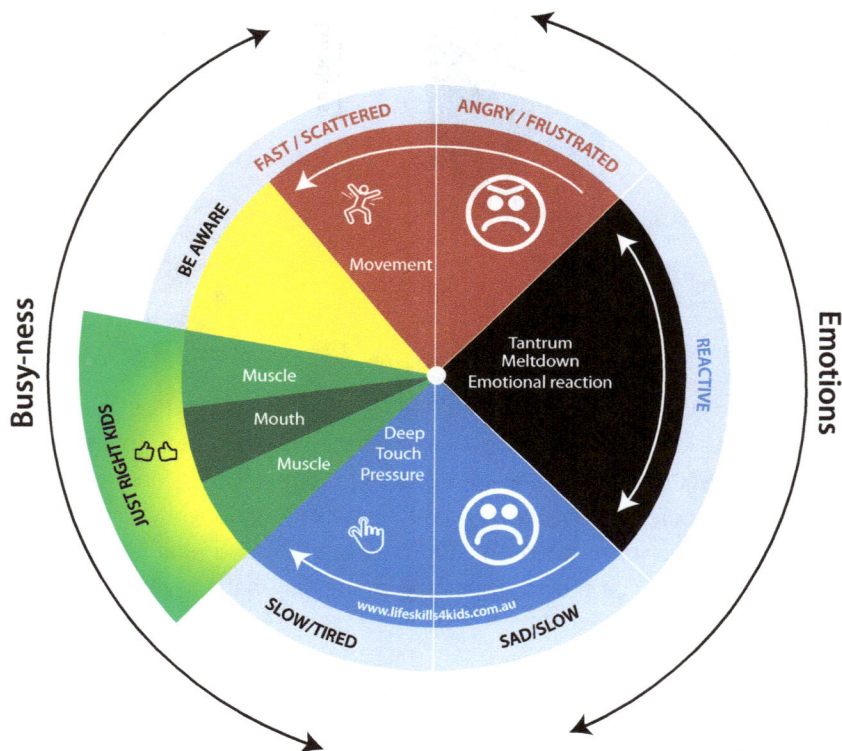

Download your Just Right Kids® model to print unlimited copies for personal and work use or type in http://qrs.ly/hd7o7vy

In this book, we will be exploring:

- the causes that underlie stress,
- 5 different types of common anxiety in kids (we call this occupational anxiety)
- how screen time impacts on stress and anxiety for children as well as families
- a bit of neuro to explain what happens in the brain and how the gut helps or hinders anxiety
- strategies for what to do to know how to help your child
- physical and cognitive (thought-based strategies) to support your child.

All About Stress and Anxiety in Children

Causes of stress and anxiety and how to identify it in children

Too much stress and anxiety can be paralysing. An analogy describing anxiety is that it is like a snake in the depths of your stomach that rears its head and threatens to crush your heart, restrict your breathing and, at times, overpower you so that you feel it might reach up and strangle you. Anxiety can come and go and it's a heavy weight, weighing down the potential of children and adults alike. It can block out dreams and make every day feel painfully slow and terrifying.

However, stress is also an important part of everyday life. We need to have some level of stress to motivate us and help us get out of bed. As parents and caregivers, we have a natural instinct to protect our kids from stress and the associated negative emotions. However, our children need to know that feeling upset, angry, anxious or frustrated is a normal part of life. Experiencing these emotions throughout our lifetimes is part of being human and learning how to cope with them is an important life skill, even for the youngest of children. It's important for children to know that it's okay and normal to feel these emotions, but it's even more important to teach them positive coping skills so they can deal with them effectively. We need to embrace normal stress-induced reactions and use them as teaching opportunities.

For many children, stress starts at an early age with separation anxiety. As children become older they may become stressed over social situations, academic pressures, and the complexities of a changing environment. Some amount of discomfort in these situations is normal. The problem arises when the stress a child is experiencing begins to interfere with their daily functioning – the things they need to do every day, such as learning at school and enjoying playtime. When it becomes more serious, it can cause disturbances in sleep, eating habits and academic progress.

The stressed or anxious child is likely to have difficulty concentrating and focusing on learning tasks and may become withdrawn. This is why it's critical for their overall development to teach them, as early as possible, how to deal with stress and to self-regulate. In fact, self-regulation abilities have a stronger correlation with school readiness than IQ, or entry level reading or maths skill.[1,2,3]

"Hoping this book gets into the hands of many preschool and kindergarten teacher hands!!!"

RG, Psychologist

The first step in teaching effective coping strategies is to show children how to use relaxation and other grounding strategies, language to describe how they feel, and problem solving and other metacognitive strategies that enable them to positively manage their stress. This is explained in detail in Chapters 9 – 12.

> 66 The problem arises when the stress a child is experiencing begins to interfere with their daily functioning — not being able to do the things they need to do. 99

We know that subtle changes in a child's life and routine, as well as being over-stimulated in new situations, are common contributors to the child's stress load.

However, those are not the only triggers to be aware of. Here are just a few examples of possible causes of stress in young children:

- Fear of disciplinary action
- Peer conflicts
- Bullying situations
- Difficulty with a particular academic pursuit
- Anxiety from fear of disappointing parents or teacher
- Gut health (see Chapter 2)
- Occupational sources of anxiety (see Chapter 3) for example:
  - Learning anxiety
  - Sensory anxiety
  - Social anxiety
  - Emotional anxiety
  - Transitional anxiety
- Sensory overload from home, school and extracurricular activities (see Chapter 4)
- Screen time use (see Chapters 5 and 6)
- Sibling rivalry

Research shows that 'parents perceive children as having lower levels of stress than children perceive themselves as having.'[4] This was also confirmed in a survey which found that 'parents underestimate how much children worry.'[5] As the child grows, we may view them as more adult-like and more mature, meaning that we may overestimate the amount of stress they are actually capable of handling. It is very important to be aware of the causes of stress in both younger and older children, as well as the manifestations; while some stresses remain constant throughout our lives, some vary in intensity with age.

"Interesting and so true.
Being aware of what their big concerns
are (ie list above) is so helpful
for parents/teachers etc.
Interestingly enough I have been reminded
of this this past week with my own family.
Thanks for the gentle and helpful rebuke :)"

SJ, parent.

The following is a list of some of the causes of stress in older children and teens:

- Academic pressure, both self-imposed and inferred, from parents and teachers.

- Personal relationships, including those of a romantic nature. As children mature, so do their relationships, and the teen years are usually a period of exploration into their first romantic relationships. These, and the turbulence associated with them, can cause additional stress.

- Along with changing relationships, older children and teens can experience stress associated with their social standing. The transition from childhood into adulthood requires finding your place in the world and beginning to have a strong concept of self and where you belong. This can be an extremely confusing and stressful time.

- Children in this age group go through many changes physically, some of which they may not be particularly comfortable with. Becoming comfortable in their own skin can be a stressful process.

- Peer competition. Some competition is healthy, but often in peer groups the competition is anything but. Peer relationships can become strained and difficult to navigate, leaving the child feeling isolated, unworthy and stressed.

- Changes to structure and routine. As with younger children, older children are also at risk of experiencing excess stress during times of change or upheaval. Children of all ages need some level of stability to feel safe and secure. Even the mildest change, such as returning to school after the holidays or a local relocation to a new home in the same town, can cause at least temporary stress as the child readjusts.

> **❝ As the child grows, we may view them as more adult-like and more mature, meaning that we may overestimate the amount of stress they are actually capable of handling. ❞**

"Such a helpful list.
Interesting that this list is relevant
for even older teenagers
or young adults in their 20's.
Been working with two clients who are nearly 20
and this stuff is just beginning to ring true."

KL, Social Worker

A Little on What Happens in the Brain

There are 2 main areas of the brain that constantly perform a balancing act to manage and control our emotions and behaviour. These are our middle frontal cortex and our limbic system. They have been explained extensively in the work of Dr Dan Siegel[6] over the past few years and it's a really simple way of explaining how our emotions are controlled and balanced in the brain. This is known as self-regulation.

He talks about our brain "flipping the lid". This may be from emotions such as fear, anxiety, stress or other reasons. He explains that our brain can be thought of as a house divided into an upstairs and a downstairs. The upstairs is comprised of our cerebral cortex, the part behind our forehead and the top of our brain. The downstairs is the 'emotional' centre of our brain, which is located in the middle of our brain and includes the amygdala and the brainstem.

"Interesting, from my own experience
that kids in foster care, tend to, on the
whole, be 3-5 years behind non foster kids
in some of these 'stressors'. I think possibly
because they are dealing with a lot of
'stressors' that non-foster kids deal with."

RF, Foster Parent

Basically, our cortex allows us to think, plan and problem solve. It keeps things well organised and planned and helps us get a lot done.

Our amygdala and brainstem are responsible for managing basic functions (breathing and blinking), for innate reactions and impulses (like the stress reaction of fight, flight and freeze) and for strong emotions such as dealing with anger or fear[7].

The cortex is the top storey of the house in our analogy and the lower storey is the amygdala and brainstem. If we start to feel overwhelmed by a situation, we feel we can't cope, we feel we are hard done by or someone has done us a disservice, our bottom storey (limbic system) becomes active and unsettled. If a child in class feels as if the work is too hard, or they aren't sure of what they should be doing, the limbic system can start to get a bit shaky and they might feel frustrated or annoyed – both signs that the lower storey of their house is not coping. If they continue to feel overwhelmed, then their 'lid' might 'flip', meaning that the stair case to the top storey is not available and the emotional centre of their brain (the amygdala) takes over. With the stairs no longer linked to the cortex, they are not able to think things through or get a plan together. Their emotional centre of their brain has taken over and their emotions start flooding out and they can move into a fight, flight or fright response.

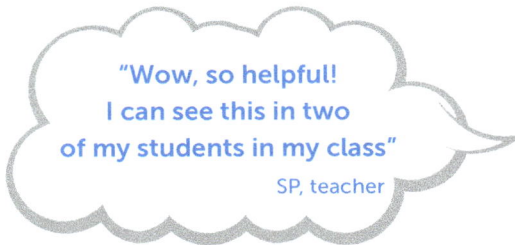

> "Wow, so helpful!
> I can see this in two
> of my students in my class"
> SP, teacher

In Section 2, we will be talking about different types of anxiety in children, including sensory anxiety. If a child finds it overwhelming to process one or more senses (for example, too much noise is overwhelming), a similar process happens in the brain. With too much noise at a birthday party, their downstairs brain (the amygdala) feels that it can't cope.

As the amygdala starts to react, the staircase starts to shake and the connection with the top floor (the cortex) is broken. Once this happens, the child shifts from being able to self-regulate and control his level of frustration with the loud noise, to being pushed by his nervous system into the stress response of 'fight, flight or freeze'. Once the staircase is disconnected, what we might see at the birthday party are different reactions, all stress responses and all in response to the staircase being 'disconnected'.

As his brain 'flips its lid', he may react by

- Fighting – playing rough or with excess force towards his friends. He does this as he tries to exert control over the feelings that are over flowing.

- Going into Flight – running away. He finds it's all too much and he might run to another room or run out of the house. This is a strategy to retreat and to find a quieter area to recover and regroup.

- Freezing – he may be in the group playing a game of pass the parcel and he may freeze and become non-responsive, or he may remove himself to the side of the room, crawl behind the couch and freeze in his body as he recovers from the feelings of overwhelm.

His reactions may form a pattern as he flips his lid from time to time, or they may be different each time. His lid may take a long time to flip and there may be warning signs that he is starting to get overwhelmed, or his lid might flip in a millisecond. This is really frustrating for parents and professionals as it makes it hard to figure out the warning signs and triggers.

"I wish I had read this book when I was studying. Thank you for this great and simply explained insight"

HG, preschool teacher

Another really simple way to think of the neurobiology of the brain (and I like simple – it makes it easier to understand and teach to parents and kids), is to talk about the cortex as being the Leader, and the Limbic System as being 'Limbo'[8]

So,

- cortex = upstairs brain = The Leader, and
- amygdala = downstairs brain = Limbo

Limbo is responsible for all emotions, good and bad depending on how they are stimulated. The Leader lives upstairs and can control the Limbo when the staircase (neural pathways) are well connected. However, when the staircase (link between the Leader (cortex) and the Limbo (Amygdala) is shaky or disconnected, the Leader cannot lead.

We need to help calm the Limbo through our sensory nervous system (e.g. slow breathing, using our muscle system (proprioception), using rhythmic movement (jumping or forwards and back movement) or other sensory strategies to calm the Limbo and ground our nervous system. ONLY THEN, can the Leader come back on line and lead. Leading is all about getting a plan together, telling the Limbo what to do or not to do. It's a delicate seesaw balance, but an important one to understand.

"Every time the leader and the limbo are mentioned I get a picture in my brain of a wobbling staircase. Great analogy!"

Peta, Mum

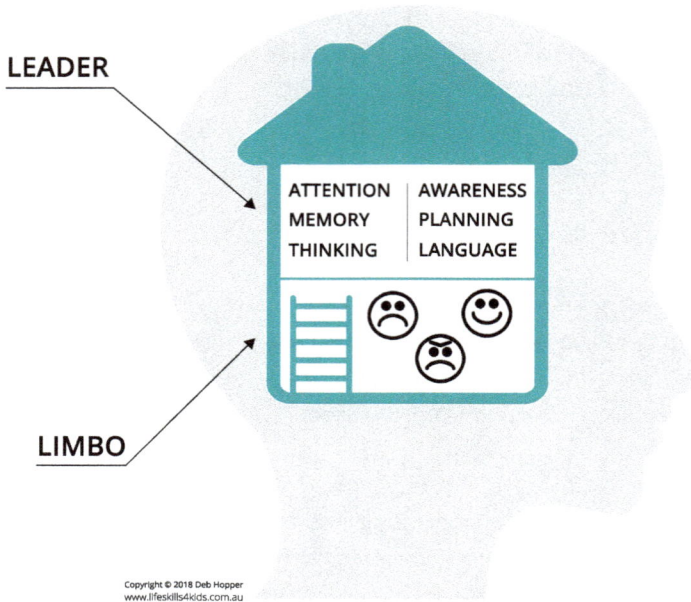

LEADER

ATTENTION | AWARENESS
MEMORY | PLANNING
THINKING | LANGUAGE

LIMBO

Copyright © 2018 Deb Hopper
www.lifeskills4kids.com.au

The Role of Memory

While the Limbo's primary function is feeling, it also has another important function – memory[8].

When a child experiences an intensely happy event, such as a fabulous day at the animal park or a special ice cream date with dad, the Limbo remembers this because it has been marked as important in the brain.

However, as the Limbo remembers both positive AND negative experiences, if a child experiences anxiety or stress, or even sensory overload, the Limbo also remembers this, and when faced with a similar event again, that memory is quickly recalled. This reminds them that it wasn't safe last time and that they need to be aware and on edge (anxious thoughts), so they can make sure they are kept safe next time.

"Yep, so true. Very keen to see where you go with this. Part of my counselling involves looking at some of these memories so we can understand our present safe actions. Once these are discovered part of what I seek to do is to help clients see if their beliefs from the past are true for that past situation only or for all future situations. Often that truth is not universal."

PF, counsellor

"I love the explanation of sensory memory. So many kids will not revisit an activity if it felt "bad". My child does this a lot. Adults are the same. We see this a lot in mental health."

Cassandra, parent and mental health worker

How to Identify Stress and Anxiety in Children

When stress manifests in children, it is very helpful for them to have support from adults who can tune in to the emotional cues and warning signs. Children may hide their emotions, or at least diminish how they appear to others. They may 'act out' their stress in ways that adults may not be aware of.

Keep an eye out for the following clues that your child may not be coping:

- More frequent complaints of not feeling well. Be aware of ailments that may come and go such as headaches, stomach upsets, sore throats with no fever, etc. Not feeling well is a way for the child to avoid participating in certain activities and situations. A child who complains of chronically not feeling well yet cannot be diagnosed by a physician may be finding a way to avoid their stressors. Also note that this does not mean that the child is faking illness; stress can manifest itself as any of these ailments in very real ways. A 2011 report found that 'almost a third of children reported that, in the last month, they had experienced a physical health symptom often associated with stress, such as headaches, stomach aches or trouble falling or staying asleep.' [9]

- Negative changes in behaviour and habits. A child 'acting out' or participating in activities that they know are harmful, dangerous or forbidden for some reason, may be looking for an outlet to deal with their stress, or just cope from hour to hour or day to day.

- As a child begins to mature, the bond they form with peers becomes stronger and, in some cases, replaces the strong bonds that they had in the home as a younger child. This is a normal part of development and asserting independence. The warning sign here is if the child begins to not only pull away from immediate family, but also begins to act in a hostile way towards them. Even with increased independence, many older children still view home as their safe place. They feel free to show their aggressions here rather than with a peer group, who could be more judgemental and condemning.

- Keep an eye on the child's relationships with friends, peers and other adults in their lives. During times of stress our general demeanour may shift, and this will be noticeable to people who know the child well. Some relationship issues may also develop if the child experiences stress or anxiety that they are unable to effectively cope with.

- Pay attention to their vocabulary. This is not about being aware of the most recent trends in slang, although it doesn't hurt to be able to translate that as well! This is about deciphering the words that your child is using. Rather than saying they are stressed, overwhelmed or frustrated, older kids may use words that are self-deprecating as a way to reach out for help.

There are a few key phrases that can be helpful to look out for as clues to whether your child is anxious. These words are like the tip of the iceberg as the child reaches out and whispers (or shouts) for help. They are the small warning signs that tell us that there might be a massive iceberg beneath the surface that is holding your child back.

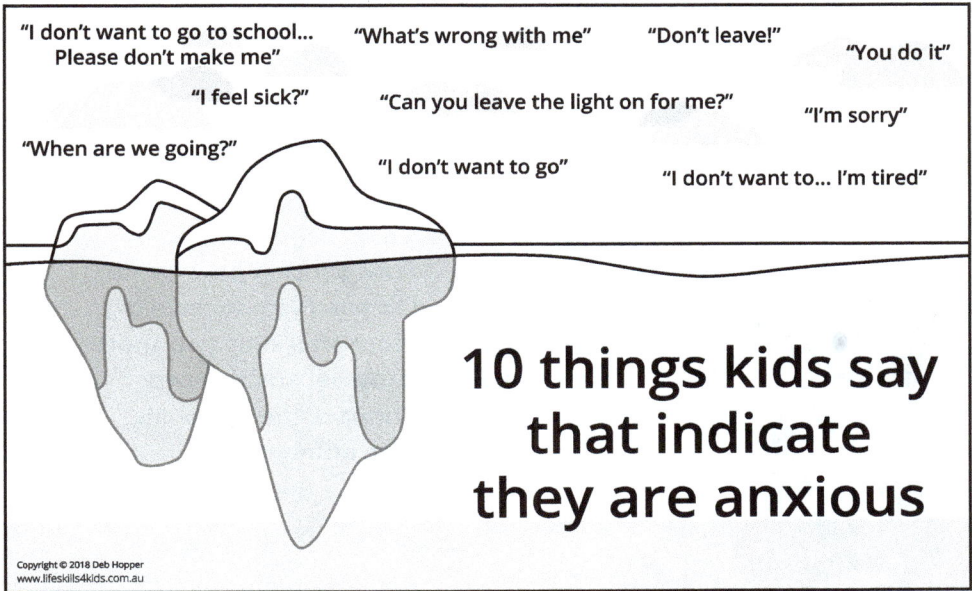

"I don't want to go to school... Please don't make me"

"What's wrong with me"

"Don't leave!"

"You do it"

"I feel sick?"

"Can you leave the light on for me?"

"I'm sorry"

"When are we going?"

"I don't want to go"

"I don't want to... I'm tired"

10 things kids say that indicate they are anxious

Copyright © 2018 Deb Hopper
www.lifeskills4kids.com.au

These might include:

1. "What's wrong with me?"

Self-doubt and insecurity is common in children, but if it becomes habitual, small worries can grow into big ones. Yes, children need to be resilient and need regular, small challenges to continue to develop resilience, but keep watch for growing signs of other anxiety triggers that might make for more pronounced and longer-term worries.

Encourage your child to believe in themselves, to celebrate their differences and love who they are. We are all different, we all have strengths and growth areas. Celebrate differences. As one of my therapy mums says, (and has tattooed on her arm) "Different, not less".

2. "Please don't make me" or "I don't want to go to school"

Refusal to go to school can come from many reasons including difficulty with learning, difficulty with concentrating, difficulty with making friends, bullying, not knowing how to play, not knowing how to go up and say hi to a friend, or how to make new friends. Often by unpacking the reason they don't want to do something can give us clues about what to do to help.

A whole team approach between parents, the school team and other professionals involved can give the best outcome for a child who doesn't want to go to school.

> "I like this. I've got a teenage client going through this right now. Sensing no-one has ever really listened to her. I've noticed a big change in her behaviour after only two short sessions where I just sat and listened and helped her to unpack the reasoning. Thanks for the affirmation"
>
> CS, psychologist

3. "I want to stay home" or "I don't want to go"

Some children are extremely overwhelmed by the sensory environment outside of home.

The noise, smells, tactile feel of seats or the touch demands of being at preschool can invoke severe anxiety in some children. Some children prefer to stay in quiet, familiar environments because it is much safer for their sensory and nervous systems.

When some children are placed in an overwhelming environment they can develop negative sensory memories which are triggered by the thought of being there, or the recollection of being in that situation when they near the same location.

For example, a child might become anxious and react negatively to a sensory memory when mum mentions that she needs to go to the shops, or when they are driving towards the shops. The sensory memory is the trigger for the 'negative behaviour' associated with a particular environment.

4. "I don't want to... I'm tired"

Can you recall being nervous or anxious before a talk, an exam or a job interview? Do you recall coming home absolutely exhausted that afternoon?

A preschool or school-aged child who has to deal with changes in routines, changes in teachers, noise, lots of people or other day to day yet stressful events, can become worn out because of anxiety.

Anxious thoughts can wear them down and also bring on sleep disturbance which, in turn, results in increased tiredness. Children often find it hard to get to sleep because they are thinking about the day, thinking what went wrong, thinking about how to solve what didn't go well and worrying how they will tackle the day tomorrow.

Many children (and adults) become so fatigued that when they do have down time and the opportunity to be alone, they may revert to sleep to physically recover from the emotional fatigue that has been building up.

5. "You do it", "I can't" or "I don't want to!"

A child who constantly has a low self-esteem, thinks he can't do it, refuses to participate, withdraws from activities, and attempts to get others to act on their behalf, has many key signs of an anxious child.

We need to step back, be the detective, and look for clues for WHY your child feels they don't want to give things a go. WHY are they withdrawing? WHY don't they want to?

- Are they being bullied?
- Do they have low muscle tone that makes it hard for them to move?
- Do they feel uncoordinated compared to their peers?
- Do they not have the muscle strength to pull themselves up onto climbing equipment?
- Do they want to play and participate but can't?

Thinking outside the box is our job as parents and professionals. Don't just assume that your child is lazy because they don't want to participate. Be detectives with them. Ask about their day! Look for clues as to why they are worried. Once you have some clues, you can help to get an action plan together.

6. "I'm sorry", "I'm sorry", "I'm sorry".

Anxious children (and adults) often apologise for things that aren't real issues, and then they withdraw. It's a plea for help, a way to get attention for a short period. It can also be a sign that they aren't confident and have low self-image or low self-esteem.

Encouraging children to be confident in their opinion, even in the small things, is so important. I once worked with a tween who had such a low self-image and anxiety that she couldn't even say how she liked her eggs cooked.

Start by encouraging a child's point of view in small things from day to day and confidence will grow in small but important steps.

7. "When are we going?", "I want to go home", or "I've got to get out of here"

Being out of your house which is your cocoon, your comfort zone, your safe place is not the first choice for fun when you are anxious.

For anxious kids, they might really want to go to that birthday party, play date or school dance. However, instead of enjoying their time, or finding something to do, they will often cling to parents or display negative behaviour or negative interactions with friends in order to get an adult's attention. They either get in trouble or make the experience so uncomfortable that they are asked to leave or want to leave.

Again, the reasons for this might be social anxiety, too much noise or too many people and they are overwhelmed from a sensory perspective or they just might not have the social skills or co-ordination to know how to play without breaking up the game.

8. "Don't leave"

Many children don't feel comfortable being left at a different place and prefer to be near a safe and trusted person. This is normal for younger children, but when a middle primary school child or teen doesn't want to be dropped off at school or at a trusted friend's house, warning bells might sound.

9. "Can you leave the light on for me at night?"

Many children prefer to have a night light on overnight. However, if a child is finding it hard to get to sleep, or waking up terrified, needing to check door locks, or being terrified in their bed for hours, then perhaps they could use some support in dealing with their anxious and negative thoughts.

Movies, stories and conversations with peers can trigger this thinking, but it can stem from many other things throughout childhood.

10. "I feel sick" or hair pulling.

When anxiety strikes, it shows up in many different ways. Some are physically obvious, others are not.

Children struggling with anxiety may often complain of a sore tummy or feeling sick in the stomach. Some children will also fake sickness and do anything to prove to parents that they are truly sick and can't go to school or can't do something. I worked with one child who used to fake a temperature. They asked for a hot water bottle and then put the thermometer on the hot water bottle to prove they were too sick to go to school.

The gut is strongly connected to feelings and well-being, even as an adult, so a constant complaint of a "sore tummy" can be a sign of anxiety in your child.

Hair pulling, or trichotillomania, can affect some children so much that they create a bald spot on the crown of their head. Another child I worked with was so nervous and anxious that he pulled his hair to self-calm and after a few months did have a bald spot on the crown of his head, a direct result of anxiety about school. Trichotillomania can also be a result of nutritional disturbances in Zinc, Copper and Iron.

Other general signs of anxiety:
- Avoiding new things
- Distressed by normal changes, breaks from routine, or taking risks
- Tendency to highlight the negative
- Asking many unnecessary questions
- Physical complaints - feeling nauseous, panicked, or sick
- Perfectionism
- Difficulty sleeping
- Argumentative (but rarely aggressive)
- Very clingy outside of home or asking for reassurance
- Avoiding unfamiliar situations
- Fatigue
- Difficulty concentrating
- Poor memory
- Irritability
- Muscle tension
- Difficulty controlling the worry

"I love how you have broken down what anxiety can look like physically and what the signs are to look for in our children"

Peta, Mum

As you can see, the ways the anxiety snake rears its ugly head and constricts children's potential, and the way that children reach out to tell us, are many and varied. As parents and professionals, we need to be aware of the warning signs as well as the words and phrases that children use to reach out for help so that we can support them.

A Gut Feeling? How the Gut Can Impact on Stress and Anxiety

There are many common sayings which link the gut to our feelings, such as 'having a gut feeling' or 'butterflies in your stomach'. When our gut is not working well, our brain and body doesn't feel well either. We are more tired and lethargic, and our moods can be lower.

Symptoms of difficulty in the gut might include:
- Constipation or diarrhoea
- Bloating
- Unexplained abdominal pain or cramps
- Nausea

Sufferers of the above have an above-average incidence of anxiety or depressive disorders. This may be impacted by tiny but persistent (micro-) inflammation, bad gut flora, or undetected food intolerances. In addition, stress can change the 'weather' in the gut, so that when we are stressed or anxious the gut allows different bacteria to survive, compared to periods of low stress[11].

This may create a downward spiral both in gut function and stress, anxiety and emotions.

The most important (and fastest) route in transporting information from the gut to the brain is through the vagus nerve. It connects to the brain through the thalamus, which is the gateway into the brain. This helps the brain get a good picture of how the body is going. The thalamus is a part of the Limbo (limbic system), which is the downstairs of our house analogy.

This is how food can directly and quickly impact our emotions after a meal. If we eat a nutritious meal we can feel happy and have energy, whereas after poor quality foods such as excessive fat and refined sugar, we may feel tired, lethargic and even irritable. This is especially true with some children, who may react to sugar[12] and preservatives[13] very quickly[14]. The Limbo becomes over reactive and removes the stairwell resulting in our children 'flipping their lids' and showing negative behaviours.

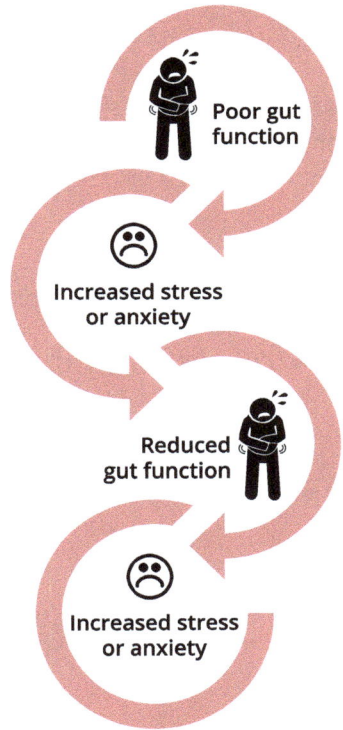

Poor gut function

Increased stress or anxiety

Reduced gut function

Increased stress or anxiety

Copyright © 2018 Deb Hopper
www.lifeskills4kids.com.au

"Wow, this is gold? Are there any helpful places to find out more about this?"
JK, parent

Sure JK, you can find Enders book by scanning here or searching: http://qrs.ly/8g7o8gv

There is much research to do to fill in the gaps in this area of study, but over the past 7 years research has indicated that there is a link between the gut, the brain and our emotions.

So, how can we help our children improve their gut health? Enders suggests starting by changing small routines such as mealtimes, to create a relaxed place to eat in a calm environment (with no TV or device screens). As a stress-free zone, meal times should be pleasant and positive, with no conflict, arguing or scolding about finishing all the food on the plate[11].

Seeking medical advice about possible gut issues from your family doctor, early childhood nurse or naturopath can also be a great start in finding out more about whether the gut factor may be impacting your child's emotions or behaviour.

[1]   http://www.apa.org/monitor/2011/01/stressed-america.aspx (American Psychological Association. *Stressed in America*. 2011, Vol 42, No. 1 Print version: page 60.)

[1]   Kuypers, L. (2018) *The Zones of Regulation: A Framework to Address Self-Regulation & Emotional Control*. Sydney Workshop Oct 2, 2018.

[2]   Blair, C. (2002). School readiness: Integrating cognition and emotion in a neurobiological conceptualization of children's functioning at school entry. *American Psychologist*, Vol 57(2), Feb 2002, 111-127

[3]   Denham, S.A. et al (2003). *Preschool Emotional Competence: Pathway to Social Competence? Child Development*. Sourced - https://onlinelibrary.wiley.com/doi/pdf/10.1111/1467-8624.00533

[4]   Humphrey, J. (1998). *Helping Children Manage Stress, A Guide for Adults, Child and Family Press*, 1998.

[5]   Witkin, G. (1999) *KidStress: What It Is, How It Feels, How To Help*, Viking Penguin, 1999.

[6]   Dr Dan Siegel- https://www.drdansiegel.com/

[7]   Siegel, D., & Payne Bryson, T. (2011). The W*hole-Brain Child: 12 Revolutionary Strategies to Nurture Your Child's Developing Mind, Survive Everyday Parenting Struggles, and Help Your Family Thrive*. Bantam Books: New York.

[8]   Morton, D. (2018) *Live More Happy*. Signs Publishing, Australia.

[9] http://www.apa.org/monitor/2011/01/stressed-america.aspx (APA, 2011)

[10] Hopper, D. (2018) https://www.lifeskills4kids.com.au/indications-child-is-anxious/

[11] Enders, G. (2017) *Gut: The Inside Story of Our Body's Most Under-rated Organ*. Scribe Publications.

[12] https://www.drgreene.com/relationship-sugar-behavior-children/

[13] https://www.ncbi.nlm.nih.gov/pubmed/17825405

[14] http://www.abc.net.au/health/features/stories/2014/05/01/3995642.htm

Occupational Anxiety in children: A new perspective on the extent of anxiety in children

The extent and breadth of anxiety and stress in children is far greater than parents and professionals realise. I truly believe that we only scratch the surface in understanding how many children are affected by anxiety on a day to day basis. Your typical child who lives next door, attends school and does well may not appear to be bothered by anxiety or worried from day to day. But even resilient and well-adjusted children have periods in life when they are worried about things at school, parents' or family relationships, and learning about the world around them and how and where they fit in.

Positive stress is important in developing resilience and we need to keep challenging children, but we need to be concerned about stress, anxiety and childhood worries when it starts impacting on what kids need and want to do from day to day.

I was introduced to a new concept of anxiety and stress in children recently, that of 'Occupational Trauma'[1].

> 66 Occupational Trauma occurs when children are so overwhelmed by repeated exposure to difficult life events that they become anxious, worried and even traumatised by repeated failure or repeated negative experiences. 99

This can often lead to withdrawal from that activity or part of life, or general non-participation across many life activities.

Personally, with the focus on developmental trauma (as in childhood abuse, neglect, trauma), I feel that we need to separate the traditional trauma concept and create a new term to describe this new concept. So, I would like to introduce the concept of '**Occupational Anxiety**'.

Occupational anxiety occurs when

1. A child is repeatedly exposed to tasks, roles or expectations that they either do not have the required skills to complete, but are still expected to, or
2. A child feels they lack the capacity, self-esteem or ability to attempt or complete a task successfully.

"I imagine that anxiety in this context would be linked closely with self-worth and even depression."

PF, counsellor

As a parent and a professional, when I consider the following five areas of occupational anxiety, I feel sick in the stomach, and my heart aches as I realise the breadth of how much anxiety impacts our children, and how often we miss the cues that children give us as they try and reach out for help.

Let's take a brief look at what these 6 areas of occupational anxiety are, and then in Section 2, Chapter 8 we will delve into some practical strategies to support children.

1. Learning anxiety

Learning anxiety is when children repeatedly fail to engage in learning or repeatedly fail in meeting learning objectives.

I see these children every day in our clinic and our schools. They struggle to concentrate and engage in class. They want to do their best and try so hard, but they struggle to understand what is explained and said in class. They often need extra time to process instructions, reflect, figure out what do to, and by the time they start to work, the rest of the class is finishing. They don't want to get into trouble, but often these kids have busy bodies and they are giving themselves positive self-talk to 'stay still, don't fidget, don't get into trouble for moving around.' However, by doing this self-talk, they can't cue in to listen to the instructions, the story or the learning around them, and while they don't get into trouble, they don't learn either.

These children rarely get rewards for academic success. They try hard, but it's easy to become overwhelmed and not even want to try to start a task. They have learnt that it doesn't matter how often they try, and because they have failed many times, they start to think, 'Why bother trying?' Think about how disheartened these children must feel, day in, day out, as they are sent to school to learn.

"So are you suggesting two causes of learning anxiety:
1. Lacking the capacity to learn and process information in a normal time and
2. Being distracted by learning (in this case by self talk).
Can they be exclusive of each other as well as both being present?"

PS, parent

"Yes, I'm suggesting that there are many reasons for learning anxiety. Learning difficulties or learning disorders do make learning frustrating for children. They may be distracted partly due to the frustration in learning, or their sensory systems may be more distractible, making it hard to concentrate and attend on the learning task. These two areas of difficulties might be seen on their own, or together. Learning can be really hard for some children!"

As their feelings of learning failure are consolidated, their emotions and their Limbo start to take over. As they drift into overwhelm, the staircase to the Leader starts to shake and they become overwhelmed. This means that they can't think through a plan of where to start, or what to do next.

They find learning hard, or feel they can't learn, and yet they have to go back day after day, term after term and year after year. Think about how we would feel as adults if we were sent to a course day after day that we didn't enjoy, and for which we rarely received any praise or positive rewards for success. It would feel devastating, and we would probably want to give up too.

> **We need to support these children to learn how to calm their worries, support their nervous system and then help them put together a step by step plan to learn how they CAN achieve learning tasks and reverse these feelings of failure.**

"Can you please clarify about what you mean about supporting their nervous system? Do you mean here to help them to move from emotion driven messages to thought out (problem solving messages)? For example, to move from the downstairs (Limbo) to upstairs (Leader) communication?"

Kate, parent

"Hi Kate, yes, exactly! If we use body based strategies to calm the Limbo, it will in turn keep their nervous system calm, their 'staircase' and communication between the Limbo (limbic system) and the Leader (frontal cortex) open which will allow them to be calm and be able to problem solve and plan how to navigate challenges."

2. Sensory anxiety

Sensory anxiety occurs when the amount of sensory information in the environment increases beyond the ability of the child's nervous system to cope. In this case, it is not information overload, but sensory overload.

Sensory anxiety can put the body's nervous system in the fight, flight, fright zone, where the cortex becomes overwhelmed and all the body can do is to either shut down or react emotionally. Examples of this might include:

- When children hold their hands over their ears because there is too much noise
- When a child can't handle the feeling of food on their hands or in their mouth
- When a child is very particular that no glue or paint touches their fingers
- When a child screams if they touch sand in the sand pit or on the beach
- When a child is overwhelmed in the shopping centre due to the bright lights and too many people moving around.

When the sensory environment is all too much, the Limbo takes over and shuts down all ability to think and reason. It's impossible to talk about a plan or strategy for how to cope or calm down when the Limbo is in control and the staircase is blocked or broken. For the Leader (frontal cortex) to take control, think, rationalise and get a plan together; the Limbo needs to be brought under control, grounded and calmed.

For children with sensory processing difficulties, that requires some intense use of the senses for calming and organising the nervous system. Your go-to nervous systems for fast-tracking nervous system organisation and calming are the touch or tactile system (deep touch pressure), the muscle or proprioception system (think pushing/pulling or resistance) and the movement or vestibular system (lots of up and down movement or back and forwards movement).

"I love how you have broken down what anxiety can look like physically and what the signs are to look for in our children"

Peta, Mum

3. Social anxiety

Social anxiety is when a child wants to interact with and engage socially with others but fails repeatedly in their attempts and/or they fail to achieve the desired level of interaction.

Children on the autism spectrum struggle significantly to understand social cues or to know how to walk up to someone, how to stand and hold their body, know what to say, and how to respond verbally and with body language.

The steps involved in walking up to a friend and saying hello include, but are not limited to, the following steps:

- Choose who to talk to
- Walk over
- Orientate body – face them, not too close, not too far away
- Smile, nod
- Look at them
- Say hello
- Wait for an answer
- Listen
- Keep focused
- Listen and wait
- Take turns talking
- Breathe, stay relaxed
- Use an inside voice
- Use gestures, facial expressions, angry voice, happy voice?
- Knowing when and how to leave[1].

As you can see, even the simple day to day task of saying hello to a friend is very complex when we break it down. Think about being at a conference or social event. Being able to approach a stranger and have a conversation can be very daunting. We need to teach our kids who struggle with social interaction and conversation each of these steps and help them practice them over and over in a positive and encouraging way. They often experience social events as awkward or unpleasant, and they are often teased or receive negative feedback.

It is not only children with a diagnosis such as autism who struggle. There are many reasons why children are shy or have low self-esteem and reduced social confidence.

> "So true. It's amazing when you think about it, how even the simplest think of saying hello can be so complex."
>
> Julie, teacher

4. Emotional anxiety

Emotional anxiety occurs when children experience repeated failure in expressing their emotions or lack the opportunity to express important emotions in a satisfying way. They may struggle to understand and identify their own emotions and how to tell others how they feel. If they feel angry or upset and this boils over at home, parents may become frustrated or upset in the moment and often feel powerless to help their child.

Children may become anxious about going to social events such as birthday parties and play dates if their emotions keep overflowing. They may choose to withdraw and not want to go on social outings with families and friends.

> "Can you explain more about how emotions overflow? Do you mean in a sense that the kids can control their emotions for a time but could at any moment break out in anger or sadness or whatever and not be able to turn off or control their emotions? I can see how this would make a child anxious."
>
> PS, parent

> "Hi Sally, yes. It's like having a bucket ¾ full of water. If you keep adding stresses, very soon the bucket (emotions) can overflow with out control as the capacity (size of the bucket) is reached."

I once worked with a child who found it very difficult to self-regulate his feelings. His emotions often overflowed at school with anger, frustration and not knowing how to express how he felt. He was often in trouble at home and school and struggled with social anxiety and knowing how to play and interact with his peers at recess and lunch time. He started to withdraw, refusing to attend after school sports and other activities. He chose to retreat to his room after school, not participate in family routines, and even stopped wanting to use his X-Box games. The effect of emotional anxiety and not understanding and struggling to express emotions is a slippery path that can lead to withdrawn behaviour and other mental health issues in a very short time.

A diagram such as the *Just Right Kids® Model* (see Chapter 7) can be a great visual to use with children to help them understand their emotions and communicate how they feel.

How to Have Just Right Kids
www.justrightkids.com

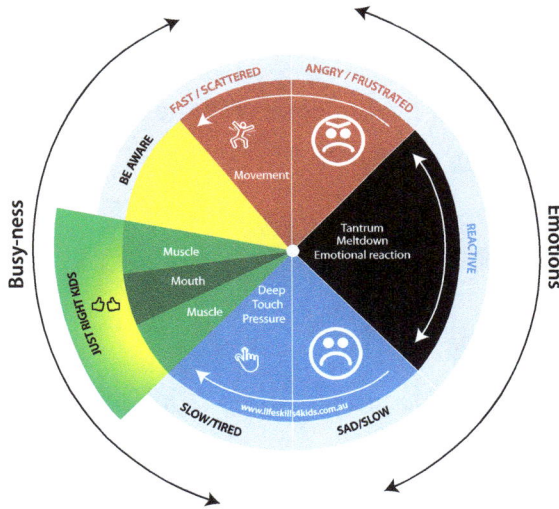

Copyright 2015 Debbie Hopper

"Do you think, like with learning anxiety above, that some kids don't have the capacity (or were never taught) how to express their emotions (hence repeated failure)? I've begun to observe that there are plenty of adults (males in particular) who don't know how to share their emotions because they don't have adequate vocabulary"

Andrew, Dad

"Andrew, yes, this is quite possible. There are three developmental stages of developing self regulation skills, part of which is understanding and expressing emotions.
    Stage 1 is where they develop behavioural strategies and they use behaviour (positive or negative) to have their needs met.
    Stage 2 is where they can use words and language to express how they are feeling and negotiate concerns.
    Stage 3 is where they can use problem solving and metacognition (thinking) strategies to identify what the problem is and strategies and alternatives for how to cope with the issue at hand."

5. Transitional anxiety

Transitional anxiety is when there is so much change in a child's routine that a stable state is never achieved.

This may occur if a child struggles to cope with changes to their routine, or there is little or no routine in the child's life. There may appear to be a regular routine from an adult's perspective, but if the child cannot process this information or cannot identify regular changes or the regular flow of tasks that create a routine, then from the child's perspective, it appears that there is no routine, and life may feel hectic or out of control.

For example, Joe attends preschool 3 days a week and is looking forward to starting school next year. At preschool, on most days they have a general routine of outside play, inside story, inside craft play and puzzles, rest time, inside play time, and then outside play. However, Joe hasn't identified and recognised that these activities are repeated in a certain order or pattern every day. He can't recognise the pattern of activities that make up the routine, so to him, if feels like every day is different. This means that he doesn't feel safe in the transitions, as he can't remember what is coming up. By creating a visual board of pictures with words underneath depicting what is happening throughout the day, he can refer to this if he is feeling worried or anxious. Once he remembers what is coming up next and then next after that, he feels much more secure in his routine and is much happier to play, and he can engage more in the activities and with other children.

"It's helpful to be reminded that the way adults see a situation isn't necessarily the way that a child sees a situation."
Mark, Occupational Therapist.

Having a greater understanding of the breadth of potential causes of anxiety in children can help us as parents and professionals, to look out for signs of worry, anxiety or distress in children in many more situations. It enables us to be more alert and more available to encourage, assist and support children when necessary.

---

[1] Chris Chapparo: Anxiety, stress and resilience in children workshop, Sydney 2016

Sensory Overload – When Too Much Happens and Causes Distress

Touch, taste, smell, sight, hearing, balance (vestibular) and muscle awareness (proprioception) – are seven important senses that allow us to respond to our environment. Our senses can deliver happy, pleasurable messages to our brains, or they can bombard the brain with fearful signals of distress. The senses are the body's way of telling the brain what is happening on the outside, and it's the brain's job to organise and evaluate the signals and create an appropriate response.

Not all children have the ability to integrate sensory information effectively. There are many reasons why they may have difficulty processing sensory input, and these difficulties can lead to increased levels of stress and anxiety. When sensory overload is undetected, it can quickly lead to distress, anger, and frustration, which can then lead to the tantrums and meltdowns that cause havoc in the classroom or at home.

> **When we are in sensory overwhelm, the Limbo has taken over, resulting in the emotional reactions or meltdowns and the Leader cannot take control as the staircase is not accessible.**

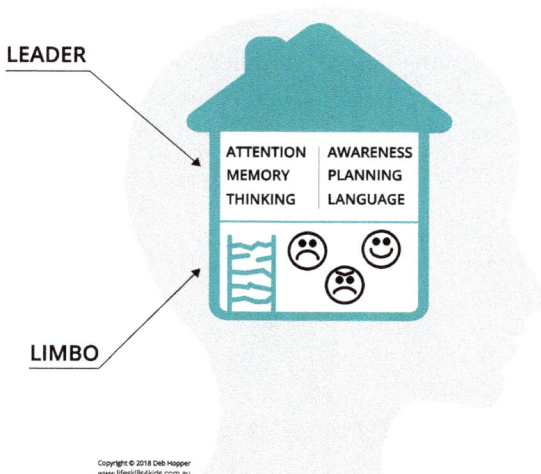

LEADER

ATTENTION	AWARENESS
MEMORY	PLANNING
THINKING	LANGUAGE

LIMBO

Copyright © 2018 Deb Hopper
www.lifeskills4kids.com.au

Sensory overload is often associated with various diagnoses, such as being on the Autism Spectrum or having a sensory processing disorder, but that is not necessarily the case. Some children are just more sensitive to sensory stimuli. As parents, teachers and carers, it is important to recognise sensory overload and support our children in their physical environments and provide strategies and resources that assist them rather than assume they are overreacting or showing 'bad or negative behaviour'. What may seem like a mild sensory experience to an adult can seem much more overwhelming to a child.

In the past few years, researchers from UC San Francisco (UCSF)[1] in a ground-breaking study identified for the first time that children with sensory processing difficulties (SPD) have quantifiable differences in brain structure. This was very important as it showed for the first time that there is a biological basis (through brain scans) that separates sensory processing difficulties from other neurodevelopmental disorders.

A further study at UCSF[2] identified that Diffuser Tensor Imaging (DTI) detected abnormal white matter tracts in the SPD subjects that serve as connections for the auditory, visual and somatosensory (tactile) systems. This abnormal microstructure of the sensory white matter tracts alters the timing of sensory transmission, so that processing of sensory stimuli and integration of information across the multiple senses becomes difficult or sometimes impossible.

Inefficient sensory processing can also cause significant overreaction to day to day events, which can appear to be stress-based, or appear as if they have difficulty in managing their emotions. It can also create difficulties for children coping in home, school or social settings. Not only is this stressful for the child, it is also extremely stressful for the parents and adults watching and helping.

The tricky part about sensory processing overload is that with every sensory event that feels way too hard, a sensory memory is created and stored in the Limbo (in the hippocampus). This means that the next time the child has to do the task, or even if the event is mentioned, anxious memories are triggered and feelings of overwhelm take hold.

> For example, Zoe finds going to the shops overwhelming due to the noise and being visually overwhelmed by too many people and bright lights. One morning before school, mum mentions that they will need to go to the shops after school. Instantly Zoe remembers the other times they have gone to the shops, where she didn't like it, she couldn't cope, her emotions boiled over and she felt like she got in trouble for having a meltdown.

All day at school, she is distracted and feels anxious in anticipation of the trip to the shops. Her sensory memory has come to full consciousness and has pushed her nervous system into a state of anxiousness and stress even though she is not yet in that situation.

In the car on the way to the shops, her body is in a stressed state of fight, flight or freeze with increasing levels of anxiety. Once they arrive at the shops, her body could react in either a fight, flight or freeze reaction. Her nervous system reaches for a coping strategy. Today her nervous system reaches for some calming deep touch pressure. She pulls her hands under her stretchy school polo shirt. As she walks around the shops, she pushes her hands against her shirt. She does this because it helps to calm her body down and allows her to cope. Today she is able to walk next to mum and get through the shopping trip. Some days it doesn't end as well. She often has meltdowns in the aisle when her sensory system doesn't cope. Sometimes she runs out of the shop.

Throughout this process, her negative sensory memories are compounding and escalating. She is taking previous learning (about how she couldn't cope in the shopping centre) and adding new negative sensory memories to the current experience. Do you think it will go any better next time? Perhaps not.

It can become a vicious circle since it is difficult for the child to learn or practice calming strategies in the midst of the event. The Limbo is in control and they aren't able to access the Leader of their brain to think, problem solve and act. That is why it is so important to get a plan together when your child is calm, relaxed and their Leader is online.

Identify what situations they are worried about and think about how you can support them to keep their body calm.

With a calm body and a plan prepared, you are set up for increased success.

Helping children cope with sensory overload can be challenging, and there is often more involved than simply helping a child cope with common stressors. Firstly, be aware of some of the classic signs of sensory overload. Many times, these signs are seen as the child being temperamental, tired or simply overreacting. Those misconceptions need to be placed aside and the following list of symptoms should be closely considered to determine if your child may be dealing with some degree of sensory overload.

Classic signs include:

- Sudden irritability or tantrum throwing, especially in new situations, or those that involve intense stimulation of the senses. This might include going to the supermarket, being in a busy or noisy place, or going somewhere new.

- Inability to concentrate or focus.

- Covering the ears or eyes in response to sensory stimuli.

- Being highly sensitive to bright lights and every-day sounds, such as kitchen appliances, motorcycles, household noises, etc. that don't seem to interfere with the daily activities of anyone else, but that your child notices and may over react to.

- Being sensitive to touch. Examples include being sensitive to clothing. Tags or seams may cause distress, along with clothing that is too tight or made of an uncomfortable fabric. The child may also avoid any kind of physical contact when feeling overwhelmed.

While helping a child with sensory overload can be complex, there are a few simple strategies you can implement which will help them cope. First of all, preparation is important. By properly preparing the child you not only reduce the amount that they struggle with sensory overload, but you can also show them how to best cope with their feelings and understand what they are experiencing. If you know ahead of time when sensory overload may become an issue, use the following techniques to help prepare them. If sensory overload is more unpredictable, take a little extra time to slowly teach them these techniques to help them recognise and cope.

Practical Ideas to Reduce Sensory Overload

- Do all that you can ahead of time and instil the good habit of planning ahead (keep the Leader the leader). Have a calendar that lists all events, no matter how minor, that may cause distress and overload. This can be anything from a large family reunion to household cleaning day. Knowing when to expect sensory overload, and providing strategies for calming, can be an immense help for your child.

- Have a game plan for stressful situations or events that might be overwhelming. If a certain situation causes sensory overload, pre-plan how to exit the situation with your child. If it's a situation which you will leave together, discuss how long you intend to stay.

This will help clarify in the child's mind that there is indeed an end in sight. Also consider the use of a special word. Have your child choose a special word that they can come to you and say when they are feeling overwhelmed and need your help. Take your child seriously if they come to you and say this word. It means they need your help immediately.

- Help them manage their sensory overload. It's important to do what you can to reduce it. However, it's equally important to teach kids coping strategies, especially as they become older – simple things like asking them for advice when shopping for clothes, allowing them to remove tags, or taking preventative measures, like bringing along sunglasses to reduce glare and brightness, or earplugs to reduce noise. All of these strategies help to empower your child and foster independence and will start to teach them how they can keep the Limbo under control by keeping their body calm.

- It can also be useful to put together a sensory emergency kit. Keep both practical and comfort items in this kit. Practical items may include earplugs, a hat or a cap with a visor, a copy of their calendar or a timer/watch that counts down how much longer they will be in the situation. Comfort items may include anything that brings calm or comfort to the child or distracts them or helps reduce their anxiety. This could be a soft stuffed animal, an iPod or MP3 player with pre-programmed calming music, a small vial filled with a scent that they find comforting, or a little smooth stone to keep in their pocket.

- Allow time for silence. We all need our downtime, and children who easily become over-stimulated need it even more than others. Allow time both before and after any transitional period or highly sensory event. Teach the child to use visualisation and breathing strategies to help them prepare and recover from any over-stimulating experiences. These will be dealt with in Chapters 9-13.

Learning to manage sensory overload and sensory processing challenges is vital for children, since it helps them to cope, relax and prepare their minds and bodies for future challenges.

Supporting children with sensory overload or sensory processing difficulties to participate and enjoy learning is important for their development and learning.

_____

[1] https://www.ucsf.edu/news/2013/07/107316/breakthrough-study-reveals-biological-basis-sensory-processing-disorders-kidsi

[2] https://www.ucsf.edu/news/2016/01/401461/brains-wiring-connected-sensory-processing-disorder

Screen Time...
The Hidden Cause of
Stress in our Children?

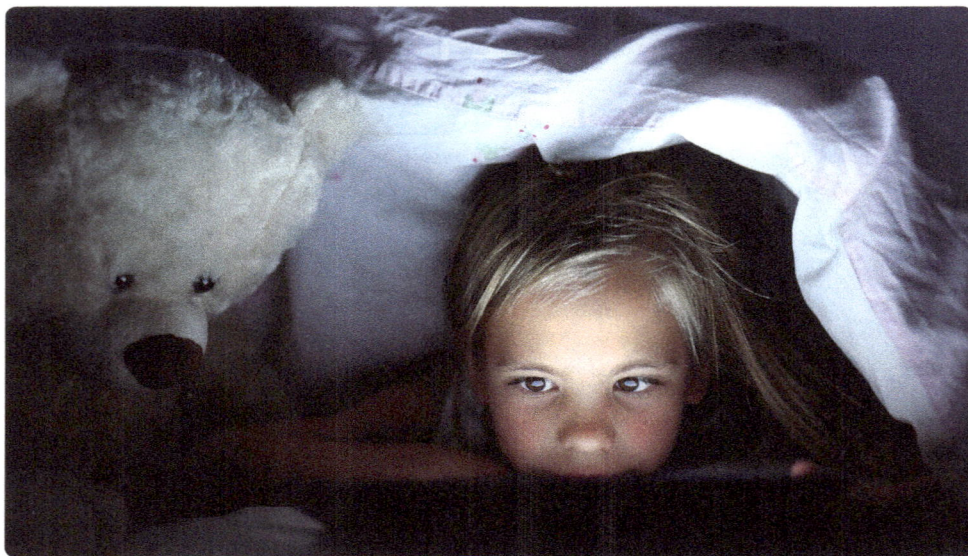

Before we delve into this timely topic, it should be said that there is a lot of controversy surrounding screen time. Should we let our kids have screen time at all? How many hours each day is ok? Talking about screen time is very close to people's hearts and can elicit a visceral or emotional reaction from parents and carers. This may be because we all have different values, and to be quite honest, every parent is on a learning curve. We all have different ways of coping and different demands and stresses on us as adults. Some adults are naturally tech avoiders, and some are tech lovers, and their opinions can also flow from this. Talking about screen time for children is similar to talking about sleep and settling techniques for babies... everyone is passionate about their point of view on the topic. Here's a sample of conflicting opinions:

- *Screen time is educational;*
- *Screen time is valuable;*
- *Screen time ruins kids' brains;*
- *Screen time is bad for babies but ok for 2-year-olds.*
- *Screen time is addictive*
- *Screen time is just the 'thing' for kids these days. We had TV when we were young, and we turned out ok.*

We are bombarded with so many different opinions by professionals, media and other parents. Let's walk through this mine-field together.

Writing about parent strategies and technology has the propensity for overreaction. Nobody has all the answers, and to be honest, society doesn't know what effect long-term screen time is having on our children's (and our own) brains. However, screen time is going to be around for a long time and we need to stop and think this issue through from many different perspectives. So, let's just open the discussion and think about how screen time might be impacting children's stress levels.

Yes, I have kids. Yes, they enjoy 'some' screen time each week. Yes, sometimes the TV is a baby-sitter when I'm tired, sick, or 'over' the day and getting dinner ready. Yes, I grew up with a screen (although only the TV was available then). I'm the first to raise my hand and say I'm human, but in balancing my mum hat and my professional hat, let's try to push these two together and get some perspective from which to work this topic out. Keven DeYoung states, 'We must realise that, as the presence of digital devices and digital dependence grows, with this growth comes new capabilities *and* new dangers.'[1] Let's try and get some balance back in the conversation.

If we don't limit screen time and create good routines in our family units, we run the risk of:

- Children learning a chunk of their communication skills and values from the TV. Many TV shows model very poor behaviour and coping skills even in shows created for children. Be mindful of what your child is watching. They love to model and copy their heroes, so if you see a new "behaviour" reflect on who their TV heroes might be or what video games they are playing at present.

- Children not being able to concentrate, learn and focus in school as well as they could. Teachers are having to resort to using more interactive multimedia teaching approaches these days to try and capture student's attention. There have been growing reports of teacher frustration in the news lately around how difficult it is to compete in class when students are being distracted by phones or devices inside the classroom.

- Teaching children that it's ok to be distracted by mobile devices, thus reducing our opportunities to interact with them. We need to engage with them and be aware of their needs. Time without screens or devices is an opportunity to connect with your children, to be there for them and to nurture them.

- Increased obesity, as children have less opportunity for exercise. Also, they tend to eat more when watching TV.

- Teaching children that screen time may be a coping strategy for distancing ourselves from our problems, rather than developing strategies that actually help us relax and defrag after a busy day. Often this is a strategy that we use as adults to cope with our own stress levels, but does it work for us, really? What are we really modelling to our children?

Three core reasons why we need to be serious about reducing screen time.

Keven DeYoung[1] outlines three real threats from too much screen time for adults. I believe that, as parents, we need to think seriously about these key points and be bold and proactive in taking charge of the issues. We need to be a guide for protecting our children's brains, their stress levels and their ability to concentrate, think and reason. We need to protect their minds for their, and their children's, future.

1. Threat of addiction

Now, this may sound like an overreaction, but it is very true.
"Taken together, [studies show] internet addiction is associated with structural and functional changes in brain regions involving emotional processing, executive attention, decision making, and cognitive control."- research authors summarizing neuro-imaging findings in internet and gaming addiction[2].

Many children suffer from sensory overload, lack of restorative sleep, and a hyperaroused nervous system, regardless of diagnosis[3]. This has been called electronic screen syndrome[4]. These children are impulsive, moody, and can't pay attention.

I have seen children who are addicted to screens. They crave it; they need it; they throw tantrums and have meltdowns when parents attempt to set boundaries. Their behaviour becomes so bad that often their parents give in much too quickly.

Just think about your own personal screen use time. How many times do you post on Facebook or Instagram and then need to check every few minutes to find out who has liked or commented on your post? How long can you go without checking emails in the evening, over the weekend or even on family holidays? Overuse of screen time is not just an issue for children. We may need to take a good hard look in the mirror!

The term "digital heroin"[5] has been coined to describe the addictive nature of regular screen time use. This may seem an over-the-top analogy, but more than 200 peer-reviewed studies correlate excessive screen usage with a host of clinical disorders, including addiction. This has been confirmed by brain imaging which showed that the blue light emitted from glowing screens affects the brain's frontal cortex (our Leader), which controls executive functioning and impulse control, the same way that drugs like cocaine and heroin do.

Nicholas Kardaras (from the above article) reports that there have been a series of clinical experiments where a video game called Snow World was used as an effective pain killer for burned military combat victims. Kardaras interviewed Lt Sam Brown, one of the pilot participants in this study.

He had received life threatening third degree burns to 30% of his body. Brown reported that he was sceptical about using the video game for pain management, but he said, "I was for sure feeling less pain than I was with the morphine."

This research just blows me away and raises red flags for me as a professional working with children who are struggling with many parts of their life, and also makes me think a lot about the effects of screen time on my own children.

2. Threat of acedia

'Acedia' may be a new word for you; well, it was for me. It describes a state of 'listlessness, of not caring'. Its psychological symptoms include 'a lack of attention to daily tasks and an overall dissatisfaction with life'. Other signs can also include tedium or boredom[6].

DeYoung[1] explains acedia very well:
'For too many of us, the hustle and bustle of electronic activity is a sad expression of a deeper acedia. We feel busy, but not with a hobby or recreation or play. We are busy with busy-ness. Rather than figure out what to do with our spare minutes and hours, we are content to swim in the shallows and pass our time with passing the time. How many of us, growing too accustomed to the acedia of our age, feel this strange mix of busyness and lifelessness? We are always engaged with our thumbs (texting, gaming), but rarely engaged with our thoughts. We keep downloading information, but rarely get down into the depths of our hearts. That's acedia— purposelessness disguised as constant commotion.'

How well does this explain MANY children in our digital world? Busy, engaged with their thumbs, rarely engaged with thoughts, flicking from screen to screen, downloading information, disconnected from relationships. Bored without a screen in front of them.

Being in a state of acedia presents a huge risk of decreasing children's ability to think, ponder, engage, learn and remember information in class. We are zoning our children's brains out by allowing too much screen time. Teachers can tell you they KNOW which children watch TV before school each day; they are the ones who find it much harder to concentrate during the day.

The above threats of addiction and acedia impact on whether kids are physically and psychologically able to concentrate, engage in relationships, organise their time, stop, slow down and relax.

3. Threat of screen time damaging the brain

More and more research is linking children's stress and anxiety levels with screen time. Most children are having 'regular' exposure to screen time. Research now shows that the average child spends more than seven hours a day with screens. This includes screen time for educational use at school.[7]

Dr Dunckly[8] has written a great summary of the five main areas of research which are showing brain changes linked to screen time use. These include:

- Grey matter atrophy. This impacts the frontal lobe, governing executive functioning, such as planning, prioritising, organising and impulse control and 'getting things done'[9 10 11 12].

- Compromised white matter integrity. Reduced white matter integrity translates into a reduction in the efficiency of communication within the brain, between the hemispheres, within the same hemisphere and between the higher (cognitive) and lower (emotional and survival) sections of the brain. It also facilitates the connection of sensory signals from the brain to the body.[10 13 14]

- Reduced cortical thickness. Reduced cortical thickness has been correlated with impairment of cognitive tasks in internet addicted boys.

- Impaired cognitive functioning.

- Cravings and impaired dopamine function. Research into the playing of video games has shown that dopamine is released during gaming and produces changes similar to drug cravings. Internet addition may also reduce the numbers of dopamine receptors and transporters.

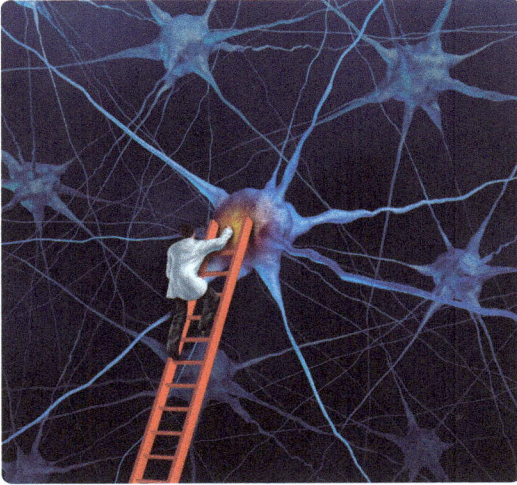

Impact of Screen Time on Relationships with Parents

In recent Theraplay® [15] training I was reminded of the 'still face experiment' from the 1970's [16].

In this experiment, researcher Ed Tronic shows different interactions between a mother and her baby. At first, they are engaged, have eye contact and are cooing and interacting with each other. The mother then turns, has no eye contact and maintains a still face with no expression for a brief moment. The infant then reaches out, coos, tries to interact with the parent to get her attention. When they realise they aren't reaching the parent, they get upset, they fuss, cry and turn away.

As I watched this, it hit me that this is what happens when, as parents, we assume a 'still face expression' as we are fixated on our screens. We may justify it as a need to relax, a need for down time. But let's think for a moment how our children might react to us on a screen.

Personally, my youngest son is just like this infant when I'm on my iPhone. He's a tween, but he loves mum time, and whenever I'm on my screen at home, he catches me, he tries to talk to me, he tells me to get off my device, he gets his homework and makes me feel guilty for being on the screen. At times he may resort to having a little meltdown on the floor or storm out of the room. Why is this happening? He's reacting to my still face. He wants my company and my attachment. He's like my little puppy who would love to hang out with me all day if he could. He doesn't like it when I'm disengaged. He wants me back and he's jealous of the time my device takes up.

"You're a brave woman tackling screen time for kids and parents! So very true in all aspects especially with no facial expressions when we are using them. Hard for my son to judge how I am feeling without my expressions. He is very big on picking up on how "nice and safe" people are by their facial expressions"

Peta, Mum

The American Academy of Pediatrics published a study on Patterns of Mobile Device Use by Caregivers and Children During Meals in Fast Food Restaurants.[17] They found that 70% of parents were distracted by their devices during the meal. Children then reacted similarly to the babies in the Still Face Experiment by testing limits or using provocative behaviours while the adults were absorbed by the device. Adults responded to this behaviour with scolding, giving repeated instructions to behaviour or using hands or feet to push the child away, all in robotic responses and without initiating eye contact. With knowledge of the Still Face Experiment, we can reinterpret this 'negative' behaviour as children who are looking for attention and to re-establish attachment and connection to their caregiver. Is that really so bad? Who is really at fault here?

As adults we need to be mindful of the effect of our involvement and distraction by screens on our relationship and attachment with our children. What we don't want them to do is give up trying to re-establish the connection and relationship. As they move towards the tween and teen years, we especially need to keep the relationship and the connection strong, otherwise they will look to peers and potentially less positive role models for relationship and guidance in those critical years, including what they see on their screens.

Attention Parents: Your Call to Action.

As parents, we have a very strong part to play as a role model for 'functional screen time'. By functional screen time, I mean, it's ok to have screen time, and there are many useful functions of screen time, including opportunities to connect with friends, both local and long distance. But my observation is that many families are being drawn into the trap of being content to 'swim in the shallows and pass our time with passing the time'.

This may be hard to really take on board and it's easy to be defensive (believe me I often fall into this trap). But the key to 'functional screen time' is to have boundaries (and enforce them regularly and consistently), have family rules, and be alert to the amount of time that is being sucked away from you by being distracted.

_____

[1] DeYoung, K. (2013) *Crazy Busy: A (Mercifully) Short Book about a (Really) Big Problem*. Crossway. Kindle Edition.

[2] KLin, Fuchun, Yan Zhou, Yasong Du, Lindi Qin, Zhimin Zhao, Jianrong Xu, and Hao Lei. *Abnormal White Matter Integrity in Adolescents with Internet Addiction Disorder: A Tract-Based Spatial Statistics Study*. PloS One 7, no. 1 (2012): e30253. doi:10.1371/journal.pone.0030253..

[3] https://www.psychologytoday.com/au/blog/mental-wealth/201402/gray-matters-too-much-screen-time-damages-the-brain

[4] https://www.psychologytoday.com/au/blog/mental-wealth/201207/elect ronic-screen-syndrome-unrecognized-disorder

[5] https://www.news.com.au/technology/online/kids-turn-violent-as-parents-battle-digital-heroin-addiction/news-sto ry/12292c2f5a1b779a56697594b871f57b.

[6] Wikipedia

[7] Rideout et al, 2010 https://kaiserfamilyfoundation.files.wordpress.com/2013/01/8010.pdf

[8] https://www.psychologytoday.com/au/blog/mental-wealth/201402/gray-matters-too-much-screen-time-damages-the-brain

[9] Zhou, Y et al. (2011). *Gray matter abnormalities in Internet addiction: A voxel-based morphometry study*. European Journal of Radiography. Vol 79, Issue 1 pp 92 – 95.

[10] Yuan et al. (2011). *Microstructure Abnormalities in Adolescents with Internet Addiction Disorder*. https://journals.plos.org/plosone/article?id=10.1371/journal.pone.0020708

[11] Weng, CB et al. (2012). A *voxel-based morphometric analysis of brain gray matter in online game addicts*. https://www.ncbi.nlm.nih.gov/pubmed/23328472

[12] Weng, CB et al. (2013). Gray matter and white matter abnormalities in online game addiction. *European Journal of Radiology*. Vol 82, Issue 8 pp 1308 – 1312.

[13] Lin, F. (2012). *Abnormal White Matter Integrity in Adolescents with Internet Addiction Disorder: A Tract-Based Spatial Statistics Study*. https://journals.plos.org/plosone/article?id=10.1371/journal.pone.0030253

[14] Hong, S et al (2013). *Decreased Functional Brain Connectivity in Adolescents with Internet Addiction*. https://journals.plos.org/plosone/article?id=10.1371/journal.pone.0057831

[15] https://www.theraplay.org/

[16] https://www.youtube.com/watch?v=apzXGEbZht0

[17] http://pediatrics.aappublications.org/content/pediatrics/early/2014/03/05/peds.2013-3703.full.pdf

Why Bother Managing Screen Time to Reduce Stress? (and some tips to help you get started)

Managing screen time can be a constant battle in families. Once screen time takes a hold, it can grip harder and harder. Making changes towards reducing it can be challenging, but it can be done. There are many ideas for reducing screen time, so pick one area and start with that; be ready for resistance but be firm every day. It will get easier.

Here are five top reasons why it's worth considering going into battle to reduce screen time.

1. Morning and evening routines go more smoothly

It's really, really common to have the TV on in the morning as well as the afternoon. I work with many families who struggle to get out the door in the morning, and most of them have the TV on. Children become easily distracted and then really upset when adults interrupt their programme to eat, brush their teeth and get ready for school or bed. By not having the TV on, especially in the morning, you can teach children to be independent and self-sufficient in getting through the morning routine. Make up a list of self-care tasks (eat, clean teeth, pack bag, etc) and add in at least 2-4 small household jobs that need doing. Start in a small way with the extra jobs and gradually build them up. Create a list or some pictures or visuals and put them on the fridge door.

The TV can be a helpful baby sitter, for when parents are getting dinner, but try and think about other strategies and different activities that your children could do for 20 minutes instead of watching TV before dinner? Can they go outside and jump on the trampoline, feed the dog or help you cook dinner? Can they make something out of a cardboard box? Make a card for their cousin's or grandma's birthday next week (that saves money too!)? Children live up to our expectations. If we expect them to do something else, if we can insert a new idea, or stand up and be clear that there is no or limited screen time, then children will test us, but in time they will respect the new boundary. Stand your ground, try something new and see your child create a new routine with less screen time.

Children learn quickly. Rather than telling them over and over (also known as nagging!), if they get off track, ask them, 'What are you up to on your list? How about you go and check the list and see what you need to do next.'

2. Your child will concentrate better at school and be smarter with no screen time before school.

Swap screen time for some active play. Trampolines are my personal favourite, but bouncing on an exercise ball, running around the back yard or having a quick swing is very effective in preparing the body, through movement and muscle input, to be ready to concentrate. The reticular formation is a small part of the brain that responds especially to up and down movement, feeding and preparing the nervous system for sitting, learning and taking in new information. Active movement is a great way to relieve stress and anxiety.

3. It's not a good example and what are we teaching our children?

OK, this point is aimed at adults. No apologies, and I'll be honest, I'm guilty of this some days, too. When adults get distracted by mobile devices, 5 or 10 minutes can easily disappear from our day. In that time, we miss important comments from our children, and often we are annoyed if they interrupt us!

Our readiness to give children our attention, especially in the peak hour family times, is very important to their sense of belonging and being heard. If we are distracted, we are not being there for them, so they feel frustrated, we feel frustrated by them interrupting us, and we are not providing good role models for the engaged communication and close relationships which we expect them to develop.

So, note to self – be aware of when you are distracted by screen time. Try to avoid non-essential screen time in the morning and evening peak hours.

4. Screen time will allow YOU (as adults) to relax and recover from your stressful day more quickly

No, screen time does not actually help you relax.

I'm sure most of us are guilty of this: after a very busy day, we get home and all we want to do is sit down, catch up on Facebook and return a couple of texts or emails. Using screen time as a stress release is one of the worst things we can do to 'recover and relax'. Screen time is very stimulating for the brain, even though we feel we are trying to relax.

The best way to quickly recover from a busy day before heading to the kitchen and preparing dinner, or starting homework etc., is to sit down somewhere comfortable and quiet (even on the toilet if that's the only place you can retreat to!) and do some deep breathing. Hold your breath for 8-10 seconds, then breathe OUT slowly for 3 seconds, and then in and out slowly for 3 seconds each.

5. Too much screen time in the evening can make it difficult for children to get to sleep and the quality of their sleep won't be as good.

- Try not to let children have screen time for 2 hours before bedtime; encourage active outdoor play instead.

- Create a regular and calm night time routine that includes a bath or shower (relaxing), meal time around the table (encourages communication skills and language and allows you to discover what happened during the day), and time for relaxing as a family, even if this is a quick story before bedtime.

- Include some deep touch pressure in the evening routine if you can. This might look like rough and tumble play, a hand or back massage, or massaging your child's back by pressing an exercise ball firmly over their back.

- Try some kids' Pilates or kids' yoga together. It will be calming for adults as well!

- Try rocking them over an exercise ball with them lying on top with their tummy down. Slow and rhythmical rocking is very calming and relaxing. Place your hand firmly on their back to provide some lovely calming deep touch pressure as you rock them[1]

> 66 **Turn off all screens for children and adults at least 2 hours before bedtime and the whole family will benefit from better sleep, increased cognitive processing from the day which also means increased learning and retention of information for children.** 99

6. You will reduce anxiety and stress!

Amy Blankson[2] talks about how screens fill our brain space. "*If we fill all our downtime with digital distractions (surfing Facebook, posting on Instagram, playing games on our phones or even reading e-books), the brain has no time left with which to process the world, chunk information and form long term memories.*"

When we start turning off screens for ourselves and our children, you will notice a decrease in anxiety and an increase in happiness[3].

---

[1] Henry, D. (2000). *Tool Chest: For Teachers, Parents & Students*. Henry Occupational Therapy Services.

[2] http://amyblankson.com/the-future-of-happiness/

[3] https://medium.com/the-mission/4-amazing-benefits-of-reducing-your-screen-time-a2c69fa0cce6

The *Just Right Kids*® *Model* to Help Children Communicate and Manage their Stress

(Taken from the book Reducing Meltdowns and Improving Concentration: The Just Right Kids® Technique, also by Deb Hopper)

There are three common questions parents and carers frequently ask in our clinic:

- What can I do to reduce tantrums and meltdowns?
- How can I make getting out the door easier on bad days?
- How can I teach my child the ability to sit still in class, listen and learn?

An underlying theme to these questions might also be, 'How can I help my child stress less and be more relaxed?'

There are the days that, as a parent, my heart sinks and my frustration and stress levels rise as I head down the stairs in the morning. I just have the feeling that it is going to be one of *those* mornings. My children are not relaxed. They are feeling pressured or overwhelmed for many reasons. These reasons might include that they are:

- Tired. They haven't slept well the night before.
- Worried about a presentation at school.
- Worried because they are going on an outing and aren't sure what will happen.
- Anxious because they have been bullied for the last week.
- Anxious because school holidays are coming up and they are anticipating a changed routine, or because they are just back from holidays and are learning their new school routine.

There as many reasons for stress at school as there are children.

From my personal and professional experience with children, I have developed a technique that helps them become more self-aware and more able to communicate how they are feeling. It is called the *Just Right Kids® Model*. With this technique, we can teach kids to label and communicate their feelings and emotions.

This technique equips families with knowledge, understanding and practical solutions to reduce stress and anxiety and thus help kids thrive, not only in school, but in all areas of their lives.

Self- Regulation

Children learn the majority of their life skills by observation, so it's particularly important that the adults around them demonstrate positive stress management skills. Parents, teachers, and educators who respond positively and directly to stress are the best role models for their children. Children who recognise that stress is a part of life, and that it can be handled positively and effectively, will develop into healthier teenagers and adults, both emotionally and mentally.

An important way of helping children cope with stress is through the process of self-regulation. This is a skill that comes through maturity, and modelling from supportive adults.

In order to model self-regulation for the children in our lives, we need to refine the skill in ourselves. Start by labelling 'how' you are feeling? For example, 'Are you feeling relaxed, stressed, busy or cross?' Then determine the best way of coping with any identified stressors. Explain the process to your kids in terms they can understand, so that your behaviour sets an example they can learn to follow.

In my clinic, I regularly encourage parents to tell children how they are feeling, and in turn, ask the children how they are feeling. This modelling and labelling of emotions by the adult helps the child to fine-tune their ability to identify and explain their own emotions. For many children, particularly those with learning difficulties, or those who have been diagnosed with Attention Deficit Hyperactivity Disorder (ADHD) or Autism, for example, identifying how they are feeling is very difficult. A child with ADHD may be going 'fast' all the time and may not know what it feels like to be relaxed or calm.

The main challenge that I have found when teaching self-regulation is addressing the two separate but equally important concepts, namely:

    (a) body speed and
    (b) emotional control.

(a) Identifying and Being Aware of Body Speed

This concept relates to how fast our body is going—it can be fast, slow or 'just right'. The speed our body is going relates directly to our emotional state, and the idea of body speed is something that even very young children can easily understand.

> When a child is acting out, they have often become worked up to the point where they no longer feel they have control over how fast their body is going. In some cases, the child is too young to recognise, or has a condition that prevents them from being fully aware of, their own body speed. Think for a moment about how difficult it would be for you as an adult to self-regulate if, at times, you felt out of control, with no idea of why your distress was happening or how to control it. This is often what a child is feeling when their body is moving too fast. The *Just Right Kids® Model* aims to explain to children that sometimes our bodies move fast and at other times they move slowly. Once a child becomes aware of this they can begin to identify the speed at which their body is moving, and how that is directly related to their emotional state. This gives them the opportunity to learn self-regulation and self- control.

(b) Emotional Control

Teaching a child to recognise and understand their own emotions is the first step towards teaching emotional control. Without this self-awareness, a child may not instinctively know when they become sad, upset, angry or frustrated. Instead, they simply see their distress as a state of being, without being aware of how they got there, or how to get back to a calm state of mind.

The *Just Right Kids® Model* helps children understand that these concepts are different, but related, and helps them learn to identify and vocalise their feelings.

Using the *Just Right Kids® Self-Regulation Model*

The Six Areas of Regulation

The *Just Right Kids® Model* starts with six main concepts for providing a common language between adults and children that can be used in any environment. Here are the six areas of body speed and self-regulation that we focus on.

1. My body is going too fast. A body that is going too fast is a body that has a lot of extra energy. A body can go too fast as a result of a variety of emotions and feelings, such as happiness, excitement and sometimes even fear. The problem with a body that is going too fast is that it cannot focus and sit still. The child may become busy, even hyperactive, and begin to lose control.

    This may be like the example of Jack in chapter one who can't sit still. Jack has a diagnosis or ADHD, and he finds it almost impossible to sit still.

2. My body is going too slowly. When a body is going too slowly, it lacks the energy that is essential to carrying out the day's tasks. The body is not able to keep up with the demands placed upon it, and this often results in it going even more slowly. The child is under-stimulated and not responsive at the appropriate level.

    Our friend Joe in chapter one is living in the 'slow zone'. He is smart and able to learn, but he finds it really hard to cue in and be alert enough to listen.

3. My body is angry or upset. An angry or upset body is one that is aggressive, frustrated, on high alert and on the verge of being out of control. A child with an angry body easily falls apart and ends up in a meltdown. When a child is angry, their body experiences different stress reactions, which might include tightness of shoulders, sweating, clenching of fists. It is important for the child to understand the physical signs of being angry.

4. My body is melting down. A body in this state is out of control and over stimulated, and the senses are overwhelmed. An over-stimulation of any of the senses can contribute to a meltdown. A tantrum often results from the child trying to maintain some control over an out-of-control body. We call this the 'black crash zone'. Kids really understand this concept.

5. My body is sad. A body is in this state when it is extremely sad, sluggish, tired and in much the same state as when it is recovering from a meltdown. The child whose body is tired needs rest and recovery. Sometimes children prefer a quiet and private place to recover in, and sometimes they like to be near adults for comfort and a hug.

6. My body is 'Just Right'. The Just Right body is safe, calm and happy. The body is going at the right speed, and focus, concentration and attentiveness are at their optimal levels. The child whose body is Just Right has both their body and their emotions under control, and their sensory experiences appropriately processed.

Kate, whom we met in chapter one lives in the Just Right Zone. Of course, she heads into the fast zone when she plays and runs around at lunch time, and she heads over to the 'black crash zone' when she is tired, or when she has disagreements with her brother. But most of the time she cruises along in the 'Just Right' Zone.

Once children are more easily able to identify how they are feeling, they will know the warning signs in their body when they are feeling more anxious and stressed.

So where do stress and anxiety fit on the *Just Right Kids® Model*?

Children relate to stress and anxiety in different ways. Some children report that they relate more to being angry, frustrated or in the 'red zone' when they feel anxious or stressed. Some children relate more to being in the 'black crash zone'.

Others relate more to being sad and anxious (the blue sad/slow zone). How a child relates to this model and the ability of them to be self-aware and know that they aren't in the 'Just Right' zone is more important. We need children to be self-aware and know when things are going and feeling ok.

Using the *Just Right Kids® Model* is a great visual tool to help children be more self-aware of their emotions, how they change, and how busy or 'fast' they feel.

Now that you know the basics of body speed, emotional control and self-regulation, it's time to take the first step in using the *Just Right Kids® Model* .

How to Have Just Right Kids
www.justrightkids.com

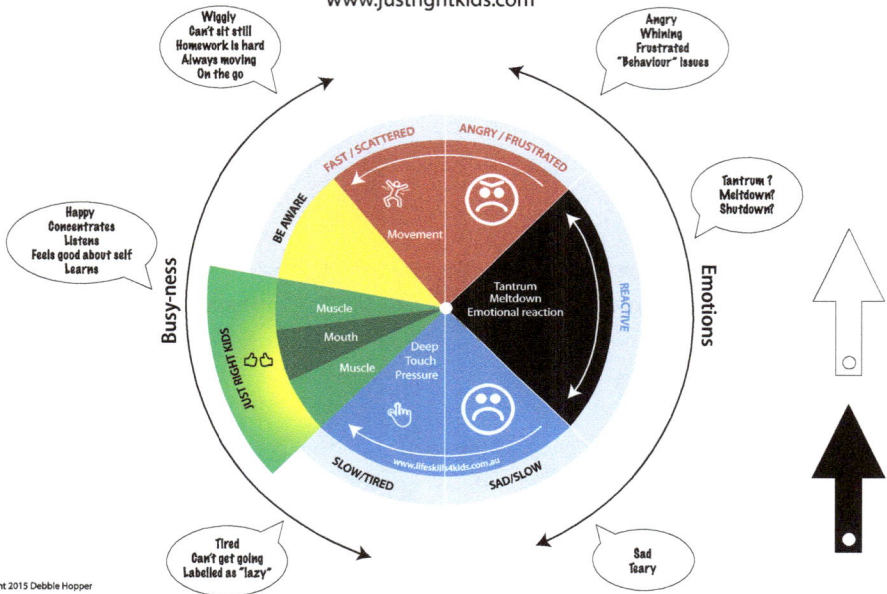

Copyright 2015 Debbie Hopper

Download your *Just Right Kids® model* to print unlimited copies for personal and work use.

Scan this QR code in
or type in http://qrs.ly/hd7o7vy

The *Just Right Kids® Model* begins with the use of a diagram. Print out the diagram, preferably in colour on sturdy paper and follow the instructions below to introduce the *Just Right Kids® Model* to your child.

1. Cut out the arrows and choose either black or white. Use a split pin and fasten the chosen arrow to the centre of the diagram.

2. Explain to your child that sometimes bodies feel fast (top of circle), sometimes they feel slow (bottom of circle) and that sometimes they feel just right (middle left of diagram).

3. Move the arrow around the diagram so that your child can indicate how they are feeling when the arrow reaches the appropriate part of the circle.

4. If they start to feel angry or overwhelmed, move the arrow to the top right-hand red (angry or overwhelmed) part of the diagram. Often when children feel like this they move into the tantrum, meltdown or shutdown phase, often resulting in tears (sad blue face).

5. Congratulations! You have taken the first step in teaching self-awareness and self-regulation.

As children interact with their world in different environments, such as home, school, visiting friends, going out for dinner and being out and about at the shops, there are many situations that they might perceive as stressful or anxiety producing.

As parents and carers, we need to be aware of the smallest of warning signs that tell us that children are moving out of their comfort zone and perhaps becoming anxious or worried. Using the *Just Right Kids® Model* and visual chart (see Chapter 6) can be an effective strategy for teaching children to recognise in themselves the early warning signs of anxiety, other emotions and their energy levels. Once they can do this, we can teach them strategies for self-care. This might be teaching the child to move away from the stressful/ anxiety producing situation or teaching them to self-advocate and communicate with adults and their friends how they are feeling and what they need.

The 3 Things about Stress and Anxiety Every Child Should Know

Teaching children three basic concepts about stress and reinforcing that teaching with appropriate reminders can help them keep things in perspective from day to day.

1. Let your child know that some stress is normal and is actually necessary to be able to get out of bed, to know what we have to do, and be motivated to do it. Too little stress in life would mean that nothing would get done or achieved.
2. Explain to your child that a certain amount of stress can help us prepare for the unknown, or for perceived danger. If we are going to a new place or doing something new, 'controlled' stress can help us think ahead and seek out information that will help us be prepared for the new challenge.
3. Help your child to distinguish between different types of stress. The stress and anxiety that can help to protect us is very different from stress that interferes with daily life. The sooner we help children recognise the difference between the two, the sooner they will be able to better control their own emotions. Understanding the difference leads to better control of immobilising emotions.

The best way to help your child is by acknowledging that their feelings are real and justified. Help them to assess the situation as calmly as possible. Have them take a few deep breaths and talk through what is concerning them. Help them analyse their surroundings in a non-emotional way. Repeat this each time the child encounters the situation until they are capable of doing it themselves.

If learning can be made enjoyable, it can also be more memorable. Try playing a game in which you imagine various situations and discuss with your child whether the situation warrants healthy stress or whether a stress response is unhealthy. For example, in an upcoming exam or test, most people would experience some levels of stress, which is helpful to motivate them to study and prepare. However, if that stress reaches the point where it causes daily distress and lack of sleep and disconnects the child from other people and activities, then it becomes immobilising and unhealthy.

Another example is when a child is alone and approached by a stranger, a certain level of anxiety is healthy and protective. On the other hand, when the child is with a trusted person, although in a crowded place surrounded by strangers, the same level of anxiety would be unhealthy.

Learn the specific situations that make your child uncomfortable in their daily life and present them in the imagined scenario with alternatives on how best to handle each moment.

A Quick Review of Section 1

In Section 1, we discussed the basics of understanding stress and anxiety in children, and some of the causes and risks for developing overload. We talked about the importance of understanding some neurobiology on how the brain works when children become anxious and the function of the Leader, and how the Limbo becomes unhelpful as it breaks down the connection (stairwell) between the Limbo and the Leader. We saw that once this happens it's really hard to recover from anxiety. We can't get a plan together because the Limbo causes our brain to become foggy and overwhelmed.

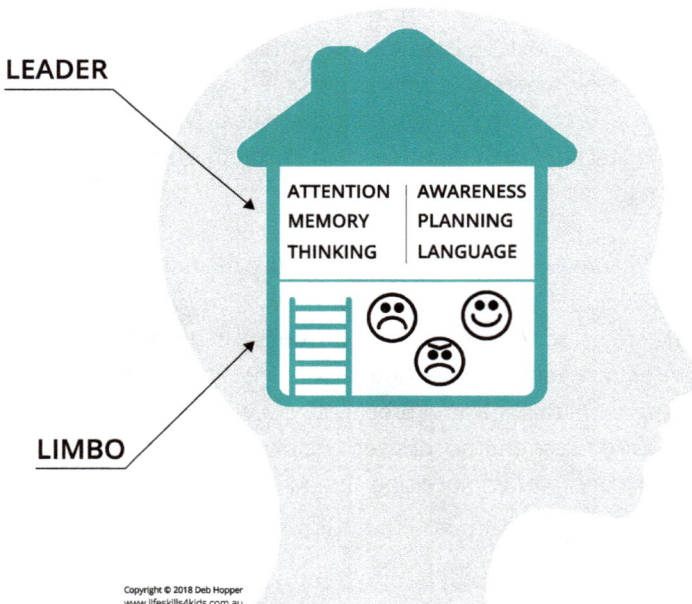

LEADER

ATTENTION	AWARENESS
MEMORY	PLANNING
THINKING	LANGUAGE

LIMBO

Copyright © 2018 Deb Hopper
www.lifeskills4kids.com.au

We introduced the concept of Occupational Anxiety as a new way of looking at when children might become anxious as an important step in understanding the depth and breadth of situations that might be difficult and overwhelming for children. We identified the concept of sensory overload and how this is another way that children are often pushed into the stress state of fight, flight or fright which is often not known and not so well understood.

We touched on the subject of screen time and how this can be another reason why children might be anxious.

Finally, we introduced the *Just Right Kids® Model* which can be a really useful tool to help children label and communicate how they are feeling and can give them a guide towards what strategies are helpful in reducing anxiety and to help them feel more in control.

Helping Children within the 5 subtypes of 'Occupational Anxiety'

In this section, we move into a more detailed description of the 5 sub-types of Occupational Anxiety and some practical, day to day strategies for managing stress and reducing anxiety.

1. Learning anxiety

Learning anxiety occurs when children experience repeated knockbacks and failures academically. It is repeated failure to engage or achieve expected learning objectives. They try and try, but learning success repeatedly eludes them and their confidence in learning is eroded.

Coping with Learning Anxiety at School

There are many stressors that arise in the school environment. Stress and anxiety can stem from separation anxiety, knowing how to make and play with friends, academic pressures and repeated failure in learning tasks or difficulties concentrating in class.

The fact that school-aged children struggle with developing a sense of learning achievement and learning independence is often overlooked as a cause of anxiety, but it can be incredibly overwhelming.

So, what are some of the factors that reduce confidence in learning at school and can contribute to learning anxiety? They might include:

- Repeated failure in learning tasks, such as poor marks on weekly spelling or maths tests
- Feeling as if they take longer to finish activities and always being last to finish
- Finding it hard to listen and understand instructions and hence not knowing what to do next
- When they aren't sure what the task is, having to repeatedly ask their friend what to do or watching others for clues as to what the next step is
- Peer pressure of feeling that they are always behind
- Negative comments and being put down by others
- Feeling as if they can't ask for help as they feel a failure before they even start a task.

With repeated failure, a sense of reduced confidence can start to emerge along with anxiety. With reduced confidence, children are less likely to put up their hand to offer an answer to a class question, and they often fear their teacher asking them for an answer. They might be worried that they will be teased for asking a 'dumb' question or for giving the wrong answer. They are often worried about making mistakes and this may freeze them into being unable to start a task. Siblings (especially younger siblings) who are achieving well at school may also start to tease which can be devastating and contribute to a child's learning anxiety.

The cycle of learning difficulties contributing to learning anxiety can be described by the diagram below. Learning difficulties contribute to learning anxiety, decreased confidence, less engagement, less participation in learning, less success and enjoyment, which compounds the impact of learning difficulties. It can be a vicious cycle that often requires professional support through the school system, reading recovery programs, Occupational Therapy, Speech Pathology and School Counsellors or Psychology support to support the child through a team approach.

Decreased
Enjoyment

Learning
Difficulties

Decreased
Success

Learning
Anxiety

Decreased
Participation

Decreased
Confidence

Decreased
Engagement

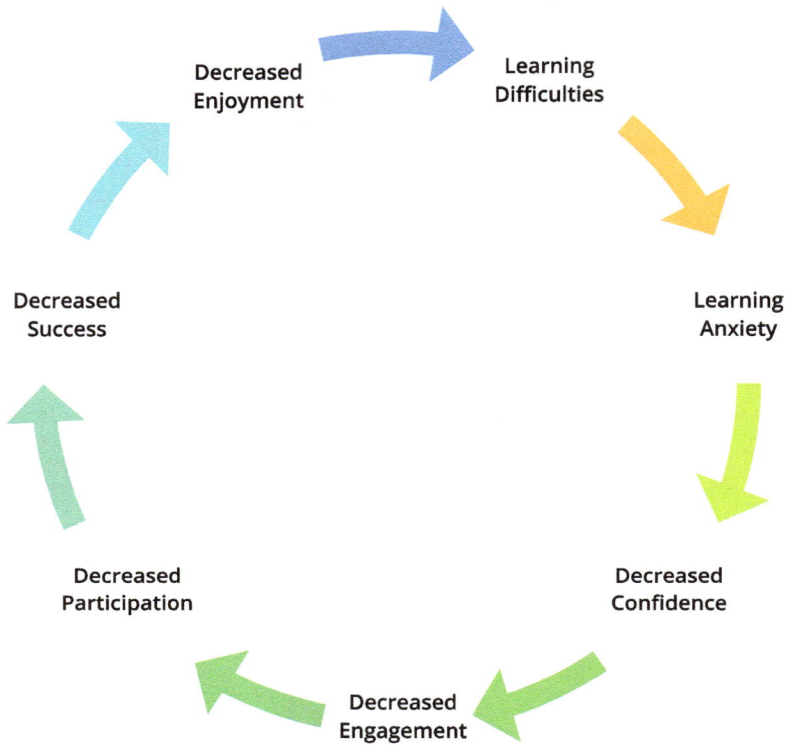

When a child's distress stems from the school environment, it can be difficult to pinpoint one primary cause, which is why it is so important to use a team approach.

As we learnt in Chapter 2, we need to make sure that our Limbo and our body is calm and grounded, so we can keep the staircase access to the Leader (our frontal cortex). Then we can get a plan together and know what the next step is, so we don't become overwhelmed. The most effective approaches to reducing stress associated with the school routine are ones that address stress and anxiety on multiple levels, and this can start at home.

Begin each day with some quiet time, meditation, visualisation, prayer or affirmations. It's important to build your child's resilience before sending them out into the day. This does not need to be a time-consuming process; all you need is a quiet two to five minutes in the morning. Use this distraction-free time to introduce a positive reinforcing affirmation or prayer that addresses your child's specific areas of stress and anxiety. Think along these lines:

- 'Today I am wise and strong. My mind will hold all that it needs to know.'
- 'I am surrounded by sunshine, warmth and love from my family and friends. I will not allow other people's words to hurt me.'
- 'I am safe and never alone.'
- 'I can do all things through Christ who strengthens me'.

Sometimes our children seem far too 'fast' to stay still enough for any quiet time in the morning. Prepare the body in the morning with some movement (vestibular) and muscle (proprioception) input or exercise. Jumping on the trampoline, doing some wall or floor push-ups, helping take the rubbish out, patting the chickens, riding a bike or skateboard— these are all are great ways of getting the body ready for learning and decreasing stress and anxiety. Up and down movement 'feeds' the reticular formation in the brain and makes it physically easier for children to slow down.

After this active time, sit down with them, give them something heavy to hold or have on their lap, and give them a hug or put your hands on their shoulders for some nice firm touching. Tell them, 'We are going to have one minute (or 30 seconds – whatever they are able to do) to sit here quietly and think about something really nice, a really nice place or something fun we want to do today.'

Just as your child needs to start the day in the right frame of mind, how they start the day physically is also vitally important and affects how they will be able to cope with the day's challenges. Always make sure that your child has a healthy, balanced breakfast. It can be very easy to grab a quick convenience food (such as packaged cereal) for breakfast or rely on foods that are exceptionally high in carbohydrates and sugar. If your child is more emotionally sensitive, these types of foods can cause blood sugar fluctuations that affect both mind and body. A breakfast that is properly balanced in its protein and carbohydrate ratio will help your child maintain a stable emotional level and make coping with their stressors easier. Examples of a balanced breakfast with increased protein could include scrambled eggs with cheese on wholegrain toast, baked beans on wholegrain toast, nut butter (peanut, almond or hazelnut butters) and yoghurt. Make sure you read the label and choose a low sugar version butter, or better still, make your own in your food processor. It's easier than you think!

Prepare as much as you can ahead of time. It's beneficial for you and your child to have a well-formulated idea of how the day, or upcoming days, will progress. Make note of exams, activities, friends' birthdays, etc.

A planner can also be used as a type of diary or journal where you and your child can record situations that triggered specific emotions of anxiety and stress. This is helpful for two reasons. The first is that when you write something down, it gets out of your head, where it can often be forgotten under the pressure of other information. Writing something down helps you reflect on, and process, your worries. Secondly, the fact that these events have been recorded will give you and your child an opportunity to look for patterns, and this awareness will give you more opportunity to either prevent or prepare.

The Importance of Task Analysis

Task analysis is the process of breaking down something we need to do into smaller steps. Task analysis is important in supporting children with all types of Occupational Anxiety, but it is especially important as a tool to support children with learning anxiety.

To do a task analysis, think of the small steps required to accomplish the bigger task. For example, often children need to write out their spelling words each morning at school and again for homework using the Look, Say, Cover, Write, Check method. For example:

Look, say, cover, write, check

1 - Write numbers

	Look	Sound and write	Write	Check	Write	Check	Write	Check
	Example		*Example*	✔	*Example*	✔	*Example*	✔
2 -	Are							
3 -	One							
4 -	Thought							

5 - Create a sentence with 2 of the above words.

_____

_____

6 - Check I'm done.

7 - Finished!

A task analysis of the above might include:

1. Number the lines that need completing (this sets up the task for later)
2. Do line 1
3. Do line 2
4. Do line 3
5. Write sentence
6. Check I'm done
7. Finished!

A task analysis of a work sheet might include labelling the different tasks or squares in order of completion e.g. 1, 2, 3, 4 and having a tick box for each to help keep children on track.

Maths		Spelling	
1. $5 + 11 = 16$	5. $12 - 6 = 6$	1. raise	_____
2. $7 + 4 = 11$	6. $19 - 7 = 12$	2. know	_____
3. $6 + 5 = 11$	7. $9 \times 0 = 0$	3. crown	_____
4. $12 + 3 = 15$	8. $7 \times 8 = 56$	4. royal	_____
		5. republic	_____

Fill in blanks	Write a sentence using your spelling words.
Australia is known for it's unique ―――――― ――――――. Including koalas, k_____ and p_____.	_____ _____ _____ _____

Section 1. Maths ☑
      2. Spelling ☐
      3. Fill in the blanks ☐
      4. Write a sentence ☐

_____

Task analysis or breaking down the task can be as simple as writing out a list of what needs doing, either at home or school on a piece of paper as in this example:

1. ☐ **Create sentence.**
2. ☐ **Write sentence.**
3. ☐ **Typing - story.**
4. ☐ **Surprise.**

It is very important for the child who has learning anxiety to know what the steps of the task are and how they will know that they are finished.

Why is this so important? Having a plan laid out for them is like giving the Leader (their frontal cortex) a cheat sheet and a really simple plan, just in case their Limbo starts to have a party and threatens to break the stairwell, overwhelm or cloud their thinking.

If we can give children a plan, the task will seem less overwhelming as the plan is clearer, the steps are smaller, more achievable and less overwhelming.

They can start to achieve small steps of success, increasing their confidence and their motivation to try again, be more engaged and start to feel success at completing learning tasks.

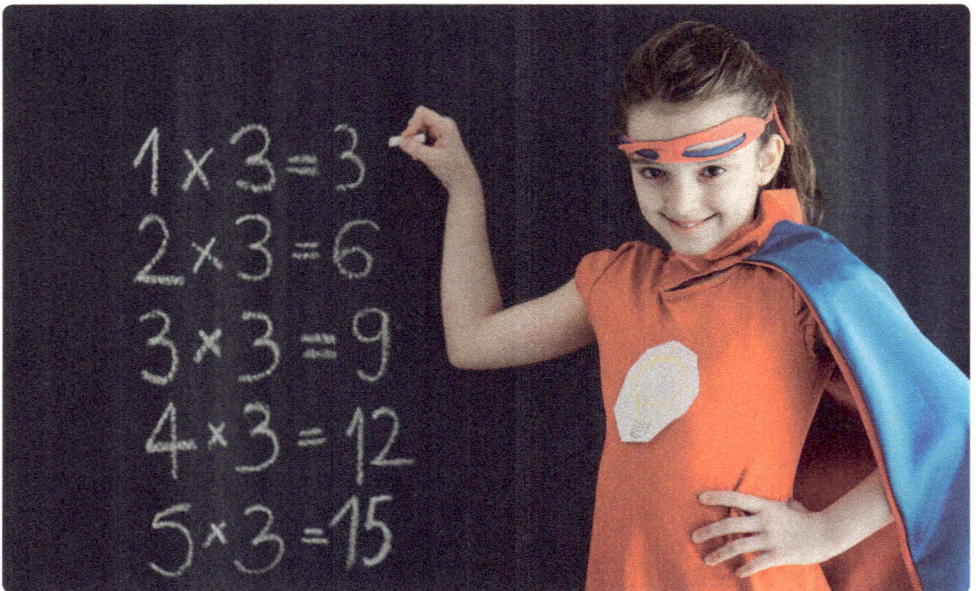

2. Sensory induced anxiety

Sensory anxiety occurs when the sensations interpreted by the nervous system are too much for the nervous system to cope with and cause sensory overload. This puts the body in the stress fight, flight, fright response. For more information on sensory overload, see Chapter 4.

Sensory overload can occur in many different environments including home, school and in accessing the community. The noise of children chatting and playing, the sound of the bell, the visual busy-ness of the classroom, even factors in the wider environment, such as traffic noise, can make being at school a stressful or anxiety-provoking experience.

At home, the noise of the TV, siblings playing or squabbling, flushing of the toilet, using the hair dryer or food processor can all be difficult for children to process.

In this chapter we will focus on three common areas of difficulty in accessing the community when supporting children who are prone to sensory overload.

Helping Your Worried or Anxious Child at the Shopping Centre

Many situations that result in fear or anxiety for your child are fuelled by the unknown. Think for a moment about how a place like a shopping centre may appear, particularly to a younger child. There are often crowds of people, almost all of whom are larger than they are; shelves and racks tower over them and there are unfamiliar smells, changes in temperature (in the fridge section) and bright, harsh lighting. Every sensation they are bombarded with in a shopping centre contradicts what is familiar and comfortable in a safe place such as home, and the experience can be quite overwhelming. Because it's so overwhelming, the Leader (frontal cortex) finds it hard to stay in control and the Limbo is totally having a party and kick-starting the emotional reaction. This is why we so often see emotional overload and overflow in busy places such as the shops.

Even an older child may experience anxiety in such a situation, especially if they have difficulty coping with strangers and crowds. If you find that your routine trips to the shops are causing your child discomfort, there are a few steps you can take to help prepare them and ease them through the experience.

- Talk to your child. If you notice that shopping trips often result in meltdowns, changes in behaviour, dread or avoidance, sit with your child and have a chat while they are feeling calm, their Leader is in control and their nervous system is calm and organised. Before the shopping trip itself, use visualisation to help your child prepare for the experience. We cannot tell children that everything is fine and have them believe us. We need to support them and help them through situations to build up their confidence so that they are able to do things that are hard for them. Visualisation, or thinking ahead through the situation and imagining what's coming up, is one way to do this.

"Ask them questions such as
- **What are you worried about?**
- **Is the place too noisy or too bright?**
- **Does it bother you when there are lots of people?**"

Deb

Some children will be able to tell you what bothers them and what they find difficult, but many can't. Having an informal chat about this isn't a waste of time if they can't give you an answer. The more we touch base with them and try and understand their world, the more they will be aware of this next time and they will gradually be more able to identify the triggers for overwhelm that might contribute to anxiety.

- Try to think through the problem yourself to identify which sensations are causing your child distress or worry. Understanding the underlying reason why they are anxious is very important so you can help them re-phrase (think about things in a different way) and learn specific coping strategies so that the difficulties can be addressed.

- Spark your child's natural creativity with visualisation. Have them visualise or think about the shopping centre and imagine walking down each aisle with them. Talk about what they are seeing and feeling, and when possible, add in a bit of humour. Have your child imagine doing silly dances or singing happy songs. Guide them through seeing the harsh lights as sunshine and the towering racks as flowering trees. Through imagery, you can change the shopping centre from a threat into a whimsical area. Create a new image that your child can carry with them in their mind and bring back to mind when they arrive at the shops. We need to transform children's negative sensory memories of past experiences into more positive thoughts that are primed for setting them up for success.

- Visualisation is sometimes too hard for children, so creating a social story can be helpful. This can be a story using words, but photos, pictures of drawings can be effective too. If your child is young or has a younger developmental level, then photos of the actual place might be needed for them to remember and understand the social story. If they can understand simple drawings or clipart, then use this. Play around with different ways of illustrating your social story and use what your child understands and enjoys looking at.

- If they are struggling with visualising, next time you go, take a short video clip of walking through the shopping centre or down an aisle at the grocery store. You can then show this to your child when you are at home in a calm environment and have a chat with them, help them notice different parts of the sensory environment such as the bright lights and the noise, and have a conversation about what might be bothering them.

- Bring a 'comfort' item. When the senses are overwhelmed, a good grounding technique is to bring along a small item that will serve as a reminder of the familiar and normal. For example, if your child has collected a small shell or smooth stone, they could bring it to the shops and hold it in the palm of their hand and rub it as stress and anxiety begin to build up.

- Give your child a little control of the situation. Shopping centres are generally adult focused and your child may feel bored and not sure what to do. Let your child help with your shopping list or give them their own so they feel important; the latter has the added advantage of giving them something to fidget with. When appropriate, allow them some choice in the items selected. By allowing your child a little control, you are giving them an improved sense of self, and something to focus on instead of their worries. Having a task of their own can be a distraction from sensory factors, such as bright lights or noise, that might be bothering them.

- Before going to the shops, make some time at home for a jump on the trampoline, or visit a park for ten minutes on the way, or have a resistance physio band in the car for them to pull on. Using our large muscles (proprioception) in resistance or pushing or pulling activities can help to calm the nervous system (the Limbo) and makes it easier to get through stressful or anxious situations. This strategy will make the shopping experience much calmer and more relaxed for everyone!

Helping Your Child Cope with Stress and Anxiety While Travelling in the Car

Some children feel trapped when they are in a moving vehicle. A child may view a car as a locked box that they cannot escape unless it has completely stopped. Needing to put their seat belt or safety restraint on adds to this feeling of being trapped.

Many children are over-sensitive to movement or vestibular information. This is registered in the inner ear and is a disorder of the vestibular (movement) system. Children with this disorder may struggle with nausea or sickness in the car.

- Help your child see the world through rose coloured glasses, literally. Supply them with a pair of pink-tinted glasses to wear during car trips. The colour pink is associated with calm, peace and wellbeing. Wearing these tinted glasses can help relax the child during your journey.

- Alternatively, trial a pair of kid-sized sunglasses which will reduce the brightness and glare and may help calm them if they are being triggered by bright light.

- Provide your child with their favourite music, either in the car's sound system or on their iPod or personal music device. If they are listening on their own device, make sure the head phones or ear phones are comfortable and that they can tolerate the feeling of the pressure on their head and ears.

- Take advantage of familiar routes. Take the initiative to point out things along the way that your child would find interesting or amusing, such as an extraordinary house colour or flowering trees. The familiarity of the route and the attention to details will give your child something to focus on other than stress and fear.

- Prepare your child by using some muscle or resistance activities such as active play before getting in the car or give them a physio or resistance band to be able to pull while seated in the car. This helps to prepare, calm and centre the nervous system and the Limbo.

- Tell your child, or use visuals or a story, to cue the child to know where they are going and what's happening next, as well as later in the day. Children feel safer when they know what's coming up.

Helping your Child Enjoy the Movies and Coping with the Dark

One of the major sources of childhood anxiety is fear of the dark. Usually we think of this as occurring in a child's bedroom at night. We often overlook other scenarios which may give rise to this fear, for example movie theatres, nature areas including dark wooded paths or caves, and some entertainment events, such as amusement park rides. These situations should give rise to a sense of fun and enjoyment, but the experience of a child who suffers from stress and anxiety will be entirely different unless you are able to help them recognise and properly respond to their fear.

First, it is important that you, as the adult, understand what is causing your child's anxiety in these situations. If your child doesn't seem to know what exactly they are afraid of, or are hesitant to tell you, begin by suggesting a few of the common stress and anxiety triggers.

- Are they worried about monsters or other imaginary creatures?
- Is the loud noise in the theatre startling and scary?

As you discover their concerns, do what you can to ease their fears without being dismissive. For example, if they become worried about becoming trapped in the dark, instead of telling them that what they fear would never happen, show them the exit doors and the lit path to the way out. Even take the child to the door and show them how to open it. Help your child see that there are practical solutions to many of their concerns (this is priming the Leader – frontal cortex and helping them reframe the situation).

Bring items along with you to reduce your child's sensory overload (which is calming the Limbo). Have a bag for the movies that includes items such as ear plugs or head phones that muffle out some, but not all, of the audio, a soothing and familiar essential oil or scent, or a soft comfortable pillow or small blanket to place on the seat; stiff and abrasive fabric coverings on theatre seats can cause discomfort. Take along a weighted lap pad, heavy blanket or weighted snake for putting around the neck. Deep touch pressure is very calming and relaxing and is very effective at calming the Limbo and the nervous system.

3. Social anxiety

Social anxiety occurs when a child wants to interact with and engage socially but fails repeatedly in their attempts and/or they fail in achieving a desired level of interaction or a sense of belonging.

Helping children with social anxiety can include using social stories to help them understand what a particular social situation might involve. For example:

- Who will be there?
- What will the location look like?
- Will it be quiet or busy? What are the sensory demands of the environment or location?
- Who will they be expected to speak with?
- Who would they like to speak with?

- How could they walk up to the person to say hello?
- What questions might they be asked?
- What questions would they like to ask to start and continue a conversation?
- What answers can they practice in readiness?
- What time does the event start and finish?
- If they feel overwhelmed, is there a sign they can give to someone that they want to leave?
- Is there a safe person they can talk to if it feels too much?
- Is there a safe place they can go to if they need time to think about what to do, or have time away from the event?
- Have they been there before? Can you do a visit to the location before the event to take a look? Can you google the location to find some photos? Public buildings, parks and schools have photos on Google Images that are easy to look up.

By rehearsing some questions such as above, we can help our child prepare for the event. It will help things go smoother, the child will feel more in control and less stressed.

Celebrating Birthdays, Holidays and Special Events while Reducing Stress

Holidays, birthdays and other celebrations are wonderful times to be shared with friends and family, but they can also be some of the most stressful for children, not to mention adults! With some forward planning, we can make these holiday and special events more manageable and enjoyable for both children and adults.

* Be aware of how much your child is taking on. Is their schedule packed with parties, events and other gatherings? Is there adequate time for rest and quiet? Talk to your child about all the upcoming events and make a plan that includes which invitations to accept, and which might be declined so they can enjoy what they attend and not be overwhelmed.

* Teach your child the power of the words 'no more' or 'enough'. If, during an event, they find themselves uncomfortable or feeling overwhelmed, let them know that it is okay to take themselves out of the room to a safe place for some quiet time.

* Develop a code word or sign. Let this be a signal your child can use to let you know in a subtle way that they wish to leave, or that they need some help in finding a place for some quiet or retreat time. Always honour the code and use it for yourself if you need it as well.

- Have a plan. Proper planning supports the Leader (frontal cortex) and can eliminate many unnecessary stress triggers. Celebratory times are often whirlwinds and can feel very unstable and unpredictable. Set up a planning calendar for your child which lists important dates and events. Also, list items that might need purchasing, creating or wrapping to prepare for events. This might include time to go shopping for gifts, marking dates when packages need to be mailed, errands to be run, or chores to be done. Help your child learn how to develop their own schedule that is spaced out appropriately to give them adequate time to do everything without becoming overwhelmed.

- Incorporate lots of muscle and movement into games and activities. This helps to keep the nervous system and the Limbo in the *'Just Right Kids*®*'* zone. By 'muscle' activities, I mean those that require resistance - pushing or pulling. This might include having a relay race in which children carry heavy buckets of water; the aim of the game is to see which team can fill up a bucket. The use of muscle and resistance activities can be calming and protective for all children and make for a happier party.

- Create a fun and 'sensory safe' place and tell each child that if they feel they need some quiet time out, or a retreat space, they are allowed to go and enjoy that alone or with a friend. This space might be a play tent with some comfy cushions, or a bean bag. Have some oil- or sand-timers inside as a visual calmer, and a heavy blanket for whole body calming.

You are your child's number one resource and advocate when it comes to teaching them how to handle their stress and anxiety. You, as their parent or carer, are the one most in tune with their personality and needs. What works for one child may not work for another. However, the above strategies will help you begin to navigate troubling daily situations.

4. Emotional anxiety

Emotional anxiety occurs when there is repeated failure in expressing emotions in a satisfying way.

Many children find it difficult to understand

a. How they actually feel
b. How to label it, name it and communicate how they feel appropriately
c. Strategies to action an intervention, know what to do or control their emotions in the moment.

Using a visual model such as the *Just Right Kids® Model* described in Chapter 7 can give you and your child a language to talk about how they are feeling. They can use the language of feeling

- Fast (busy, hyperactive, mind racing)
- Slow (tired)
- Just right – feeling great, happy, calm
- Angry
- Meltdown or black crash zone
- Sad

Helping your child when they feel upset

Creating a social story or a checklist can help a child with emotional anxiety to feel validated that sometimes they do get worried or upset, and it allows them to start to learn the name of the emotion in that situation. Once they have language for an emotion and they are more aware of how their body feels for that emotion, then they are more able to start to tell us how they feel.

> ❝ **Teaching children to recognise and label emotions is one of the hardest tasks to support and teach them, but once they get it, they can move towards learning strategies for self-regulation.** ❞

Here's a social story I created recently with one of my Year 1 girls to help give her strategies to know what to do when she got upset. As you read this, have a think about whether we are talking about the Leader or the Limbo in the story.

What to do when I get upset
By_____ and Deb Hopper

Sometimes I feel worried and sometimes I get upset and mad.

Upset

Mad

My body feels different.

My heart beats really fast.

My breathing gets fast too.

My fingers scratch my arms or my legs or my head. This feels better for a bit but sometimes I bleed and see blood but then it hurts. This is not good.

When I feel like this, I can tell myself and mum / dad or my teacher that I feel upset or sad or worried.

Talk to an adult

There are things I can do to help slow my heart, slow my breathing and not scratch. This will help me get back to the green and happy zone really fast.

I can do some drawing.

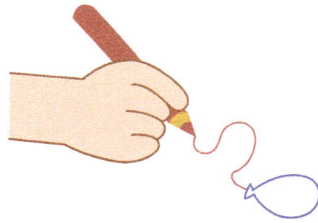

I can do 5 deep breaths

I can stretch my arms and legs

I can ask for a hug

By doing these things
I can make my body
feel happy quickly.

The first part of story describes the effects of the Limbo being in control. It's the physical reactions – the breathing, heart rate and the need to scratch. After this we list the plan of how things could be done differently next time so that she can keep her body calm and organised, keeping the Limbo under control and letting the Leader be the leader of the Limbo.

5. Transitional anxiety

Transitional anxiety is when there is repeated change in a child's routine, or not enough 'perceived' stability or routine for the child to understand what the routine is, what's coming up next. Because of this, they may feel like there is no stability in their routine when transitions occur and they are anxious because of this.

Transitional anxiety also includes children who struggle when changing from one activity to another and struggle with processing when the transition is going to happen, what the transition is, what they need to do during the transition and what activity they are transitioning to.

For example, the task of getting organised when a child arrives at school, putting their bag away and getting organised within the classroom morning routine. A task analysis of this routine might include:

- Line up with class
- Walk to classroom
- Put bag in place
- Get fruit out of bag for fruit break
- Get homework folder out of bag
- Walk into classroom
- Put fruit on desk
- Put homework in homework tub
- Sit on floor ready for roll call.

It may appear that a child knows the routine, but it might be helpful for a child who struggles with Transition Anxiety to have a list (either words or visuals) or a social story and to have this read to them before they go to school or have their list or visuals with them so they can check if they aren't sure and to reduce their level of anxiety. Children do use other coping strategies such as watching other kids and checking what the next step is.

"Not all children need the most supportive level of strategies, but it's helpful to take a step back and consider the complexity of routines" Deb

As a parent, teacher, therapist team, look at other strategies and methods for supporting children if the anxiety continues.

Helping Your Child Transition to a New School

Transitioning a child to a new school or new school campus is a task that takes up many hours in my diary as an Occupational Therapist, for preparation in term 4 and for implementation in term 1.

Generally, I follow the process of

1. Preparation – before the onsite orientation:
   a. How is the child feeling about visiting their new school for the first time?
   b. What fears or worries do they have?
   c. Are they excited or worried?
   d. I often help them express how they are feeling using emotion cards, counters using The Zones of Regulation® language and colours, or through creative means such as creating images of their emotions through drawing, painting or playdoh.
2. On site orientation:
   a. Meeting the child and parent outside the school 10 minutes before the orientation at the new school to check in with how they are feeling.
   b. Being a part of the orientation and taking photos for remembering what different parts of the school look like
   c. Creating a social story with the photos from the orientation session. We describe the physical environment as well as writing about how they felt about the visit and different parts of the new school.
3. Second or third onsite visits:
   a. Spending time in the actual classroom they will be in for a couple of classes is really important in helping children transition. This allows the child to feel more comfortable with the new classroom, including all aspects of the sensory environment such as the visual environment, sounds, echoes, smells, the sounds of the bell ringing and how the children transition from line up to the classroom.

Doing this the term before the transition is required provides a solid basis for transitioning children who may be very anxious or who may be at risk of self-regulation or emotional reactions when they are out of routine. Often children with autism (ASD) are the children who benefit the most from these transition programs, but all children benefit from doing transition programs.

---

[1] Kuypers, L. (2011). *The Zones of Regulation: A Curriculum Designed to Forster Self-regulation and Emotional Control.*

We can look at teaching tools and strategies for reducing stress and anxiety in both children and adults from two different perspectives. They can be described as top-down (cognitive or thinking strategies) or bottom-up (or body work/ muscle/physical) approaches.

Using our analogy of the Leader and the Limbo, top-down cognitive strategies support the Leader in getting a plan together, and bottom-up strategies support the Limbo to stay calm and grounded, which allows the Leader to do its job.

Teaching children a combination of these techniques provides the best support and gives more options to discover what works for different children. In this chapter, we will outline a few examples of each approach.

S-M-I-L-E-R-S

S-M-I-L-E-R-S is a combination of bottom up (body based calming strategies) and top down (thinking or cognitive strategies).

S-M-I-L-E-R-S are a group of scientifically proven ways of improving not just your children's moods, but also your own. Recently I came across the book *Live More Happy* by Dr Darren Morton[1]. It is one of the best and most easily understood resources I have found for helping us understand the impact of the frontal cortex (Leader), the Limbo (limbic system) and the effects on anxiety and conversely happiness.

He talks about practical strategies throughout his book, which he summarises under the acronym S-M-I-L-E-R-S, and then backs up his strategies with the latest research. I love his book so much, that I'm very happy to share the direct link with you here http://qrs.ly/pz7ogrh.

In this chapter, and thanks to Darren for allowing me to share, I will give an overview of the concept of the S-M-I-L-E-R-S strategies, but from the perspective of helping children. However, I highly recommend you get your hands on a copy of his *Live More Happy*[1] book.

S – Speak Positively

You have probably heard about the concept of positive self-talk and believing in yourself. But how and why is this so important?

We have talked in previous chapters about how important it is that our Leader (pre-frontal cortex) is in control most of the time and how the Limbo tries to hijack the Leader and take control. When we speak positively towards ourselves and others, our brain is building up reinforcements for our staircase, or neuro pathways between the Leader and the Limbo. This keeps the Leader strong and in control of our emotions, our motivation and our positive choices. The Leader contains speech and language areas which are linked to the Limbo and which can impress and change the emotions and mood of the Limbo quite easily, both positively and negatively.

Think about a time when you felt tired and like you were coming down with the flu. If you talk to yourself with words or self-talk such as, "I think I'm going to get sick," chances are you will probably feel worse, not go to work and feel miserable all day because you have told yourself you are sick. On the flip-side, if you use your Leader to take charge and re-frame your thinking, you might say, "I'm feeling a bit fragile, but I'll go to work and I'm sure I'll feel better soon," then at least you will be at work and chances are you'll see the day through. If not, you really are sick and it's OK to go home and rest.

For children experiencing anxiety, helping them to rephrase their anxious thoughts is extremely important but they will need your support as an adult to do it to start with. When a child is anxious and feels totally overwhelmed, their Limbo has taken over. After helping their body feel grounded, we can help children to reframe and break down their anxious thoughts into achievable steps. For example, if they have to participate in a school speech in class, we can help structure the task so they can

1. Feel calmer before they start
2. Help them to know what to say
3. Give them strategies for saying positive self-talk (I can do this, I'm going to try my best, I did well)
4. Break down the task for them – practice each paragraph of the speech separately, so they experience success, and
5. Encourage them to have positive self-talk and affirmations after their practice or speech.

> **"For children experiencing anxiety, helping them to rephrase their anxious thoughts is extremely important by they will need your support as an adult to do it at first"**
> Deb

M – Move Dynamically

Movement is such an important part of life. After movement, whether it's a walk around the block, a bike ride, or even just using the stairs instead of the lift, we feel more alert, calmer and able to think more clearly. Movement helps to support the staircase between the Leader and the Limbo and helps to keep the Leader in control and thinking clearly for us. The thing is, when we are stressed or anxious our Limbo takes over and is in control, often pushing our nervous system into a state of **flight**, **flight** or **freeze**. When we are in this state, we don't feel like going for a walk. This is where it's great to have a support person to encourage us to get up and move.

For our children, we are their cheer leader and their coach. When they are in a state of anxiety, they won't feel like getting up and moving either. It's up to us to know and understand what they enjoy doing and use their interests to help motivate them to move in some way. This concept of using their roles, habits and interests is vitally important.

In sections 1 and 2 we talked about the concept of Occupational Anxiety. Yes, anxiety is prevalent in some of the different roles in which our children need to participate, but it is a really effective strategy to use a child's occupation as a practical way of incorporating activities into their day to reduce anxiety. Adding occupation (roles, habits, routines, interests) gives additional meaning to life and a sense of purpose which can act towards developing protective factors and promoting resilience in children.

So why is movement so important? I love this quote:

> 66 **We are what we eat, and we live what we sense. By controlling what we take in through our senses, we can influence how we feel, what we think and how we behave.** 99 [2]

By controlling what we take in through our movement and muscle system, we can change the way we feel, including our level of anxiety. How is this so? Our brain needs to get information from all around our body to know where it is, so it can work in a co-ordinated way, so we can move up steps without having to look at every step or being able to type without looking at every key. This happens though our proprioceptive system. This is the system that senses information about where our body parts are without us having to look all the time.

When the Leader receives information from our muscle or proprioceptive system, the messages pass directly through the Limbo on the way to the Leader. The result is that motion creates emotion as the proprioceptors tell the Limbo how to feel[3] (LeDoux, 1998; Morton 2018). How amazing is this? That is why using our muscles or movement in daily tasks that are meaningful for us helps create a sense of calm and organisation. For example, if a child enjoys jumping on the trampoline, they are getting really strong sensory input through both the proprioceptors and their movement (vestibular) system. If they also feel like it is fun, they enjoy it and this leisure 'occupation' is more meaningful to this child, compared to one who doesn't enjoy trampolining.

It is vitally important to encourage children to engage in meaningful activities (occupations) when working out what activities they can use to keep the Limbo cool and calm.

So apart from movement, how else can we sooth our Limbo using our proprioceptors?

The 3-S approach is a great way for kids (and adults) to keep ourselves cool, calm and collected.

The 3-S approach[1]

1. Slow – Slow breathing. When we are anxious, we develop slow, rapid breathing. By slowing down the rate of our breathing and taking deeper breaths, we can feed and calm our Limbo, allowing our leader to take control. Age appropriate strategies for kids might include:

   - blowing bubbles or blowing out candles
   - using visualisation for slow breathing e.g. imagining filling their lungs like a balloon, and
   - blowing up balloons.

2. Sip – Simply wetting our mouths can be helpful in stimulating the proprioceptors to the Limbo, providing calming input. To make this input more effective, choose a drink bottle that requires a firm suck so that the mouth muscles make a nice seal around the top of the drink bottle (like a pop-top drink bottle) or a straw. Straws also need a lot more mouth movements and pressure to drink from and give lots of nice proprioception to the limbic system.

3. Sink – this refers to what we do with our muscles and again is a proprioception strategy. Sinking is like a conscious muscle release. When we are stressed or anxious, our muscles tighten and tense up as we get ready for the fight, flight or freeze reaction to protect ourselves. Sinking is the process of being aware of the muscle tension in our bodies, and practicing releasing this tightness by making our muscles feel heavier. We often do this automatically when we sink into the lounge at night to relax. As we relax our muscles by sinking, we also slow down our breathing which assists in further tension release.

I – Immerse in an Uplifting Physical Environment

66 During every moment of our life we experience the world through our varied sensory systems. Sensory experiences drive our behaviour and contribute to the organisation of our thoughts and emotions. 99 [4]

The environment in which we live and work can directly impact how we feel. Our environments are full of sensory rich information including sight, noise, touch, taste, smell etc. The mixture of these different sensory elements can directly change how we feel through the information that is sent through the Limbo to the Leader, as we have learnt.

If the restaurant we are eating in is too noisy, it can be distracting or painful to our auditory system and impact on our emotions, making us feel anxious, frustrated or drained. I remember eating at a popular restaurant at Darling Harbour (Sydney) recently and I measured the noise level at 90 dB with general chatter and at over 110 dB when they sang happy birthday! It was intense, draining and too hard to have a conversation!

It's the same for children who are sensitive to noise. Even though classroom noise isn't that extreme, they can find the chatter of other children annoying, frustrating and draining.

The cheat sheet for reducing anxiety using our environment is to get outside in nature. Nature has its own rhythm of sound and music – the wind in the trees, the crashing of the waves or gurgling of a stream. Nature is God's pace for an organised life and we all need to escape the man-made noise of our homes, workspaces and traffic to rejuvenate in the rhythm of nature.

In our current society, breaking outdoors and being exposed to natural light is extremely important for reinforcing good sleep routines and melatonin production that will help us get to and stay asleep. Being exposed to the blue light of the early morning is also extremely important for stimulating our brains so we can become alert and ready for the day's activity. Conversely, reducing artificial blue light exposure from screen use at night time is imperative for being able to relax and achieve a deep sleep.

The Limbo lights up and responds to bright light and natural landscapes and the sun is the best source of light to light up the limbo. LUX is the measurement of the intensity of light. There has been research on the best intensity of light in classrooms[5]. The Clever Classrooms report from the University of Salford (UK) found that 'of all the design parameters considered (for enhancing learning), that lighting has the strongest individual impact. The most important issues were to include as much natural light as possible, reduce the glare from natural sunlight and to include good quality electrical lighting to supplement classroom illumination.

The consensus is that we need about 30 minutes per day of exposure to 10 000 LUX to lift our Limbo and feel happier.[6] So how can we help our children achieve this and help reduce their anxiety? Indoor light is about 300 - 500 LUX. A natural sunlight beam can be 100 000 LUX, and in the shade on a bright sunny day, our eyes can be immersed in about 25 000 LUX. So, even when we are encouraging children to stay in the shade in summer, they are receiving enough LUX input to increase mood at recess and lunch. Imagine the benefit of reduced anxiety and increased mood if your child could have more outside time before and after school!

L – Look to the Positive

Let's think back for a minute to our picture of the Leader and the Limbo. Remember that the Leader and Limbo are linked to each other via the staircase or the neurons, that send messages to and from. If the Leader is in charge, it can send our thoughts (positive or negative) to the Limbo to tell it what emotions it wants us to have. If we need to do a 10-minute talk at a work meeting, for example, our Leader can relay a couple of different scenarios to the Limbo.

1. It might say, "This talk is going to be really nerve racking. I don't know if you can do it Deb; maybe you should pull out or stay home 'sick'".
2. Or, it might say, "This talk is new. You've prepared well, you have your PowerPoint slides and notes. It's normal to be nervous, but just go in and do your very best. It will be OK."

How do you think you would feel after these two different reactions? In the first scenario, I think I'd be feeling sick in the tummy, nervous, maybe have a little diarrhea and shallow breathing. The Limbo would be put on alert and react, creating fireworks and pulling the stairwell from the Limbo, reducing access to the Leader, which would make it very hard for the Leader to get back in control with more positive thoughts.

However, if your Leader is strong and you choose to focus on a positive slant, as in scenario 2, your Leader would send messages to the Limbo that all is OK and under control. It would tell your leader to keep the calm and positive thoughts flowing and the staircase between the Leader and Limbo would continue to be strong and open for clear communication. The Leader would stay in control!

We need to say many positive words to our children! We need to be encouraging and nurturing in our interactions. Negative words stimulate the Limbo and, consequently, negative reactions. In anxious children, their Limbo is already on high alert if not already in charge, and the staircase link to the Leader (frontal cortex) is shaky.

> 66 Children (especially those who are anxious) need to hear positive and encouraging words. Positive words support their Leader (frontal cortex) and help them take back control and learn to lead their own thoughts to be more positive. 99

It is our role as parents, carers and professionals to be very mindful of using positive language with children. Adults need to encourage children to change their words if their words or self-talk are not positive. This is an important life skill that can be life changing! Negative self-talk patterns create thicker and faster neurons between the Leader and the Limbo. These negative self-talk patterns are harder to change the more they are reinforced. We need to support children to change negative self-talk as a priority and be mindful that our words are positive, as children mimic and look to us for what to say and do.

E – Eat Nutritiously

Many children and families struggle to find the balance with eating nutritiously. Many of our foods are not actually nutritious but are food-like substances (Pollen 3). The families of children with anxiety that I work with often face the additional burden of a child who is a picky or problem eater (eating less than 20 foods) as well as often having a diagnosis of Autism Spectrum Disorder (ASD), Attention Deficit Hyperactivity Disorder (ADHD) or other developmental issues.

In Chapter 2 we spoke about the importance of eating gut-friendly food and the direct impact this has on our emotions. This is so important to understand! With direct links between the gut and the Limbo, what we eat can change how we feel. What a simple way to support our children out of anxiety and towards being calmer, more relaxed and happier.

If your child is struggling with eating, it's really important to seek professional help. There are various professionals with different viewpoints who work to support picky and problem eaters including dietitians, occupational therapists, speech pathologists and psychologists. There are also different programs, such as the SOS (Sensory Oral Sequencing) Fussy Eating Program[7] that assesses children from a wholistic viewpoint to find out the underlying reasons WHY they are struggling. This program then assists them in improving mouth movements, supporting their posture while eating, dealing with the sensory side, working through suggestions and strategies for supporting the psychology of eating.

So why is it so important to encourage our children to eat nutritious food and how does it affect our emotions? Dr Darren Morton1 describes an interesting viewpoint about the link to food and mood. He describes our immune system as being an incredibly sophisticated inbuilt line of defence for dealing with bugs (bacteria or virus). While our immune system is fighting off these bugs, our body needs to

1. Conserve energy (as it takes internal energy to fight off the bugs). This might look like us being tired or lethargic when we have the flu.
2. Stay away from other people to prevent bugs from spreading.

Now consider some of the signs of anxiety and depression – tiredness, lethargy and wanting to stay away from people. It sounds similar, doesn't it?

Food-like substances are packaged and can be usually be found in the middle aisle of the supermarket. As a rule of thumb, if our great-great-grandma wouldn't recognise it as food, then our body doesn't either. It sees it as a foreign invader. The result is that our body goes into defence and depressed mode many times a day.

What does this mean for our children? Whenever children consume food-like substances, their immune system is challenged.

Many children are given food-like or packaged foods for:

- breakfast (sugary breakfast cereals, white bread and sugary spreads),
- recess (muesli bars or other packaged treats),
- lunch (canteen food, white bread, packaged chips),
- after school (whatever is in the cupboard) and
- dinner (chicken nuggets, chips, takeaway etc).

Now, not all children eat like this, but many do to some degree and I'm certain that most children have a mixture of the above at some time throughout the week.

There are many and complex reasons for this, but some include:

- children with autism spectrum disorders or other disabilities who are problem eaters and prefer the white, plain, sugary or salty foods
- parents who struggle with picky or problem eaters
- or everyday parents who are busy, trying to juggle the balls of life themselves and are just trying to cope from day to day. This seems to include most of us in some way doesn't it?

So how do we support kids with great nutrition? Many studies now show a strong connection between plant-based diets and positive mood[1][9][10][11][12] (6) It is so important to increase fruit and vegetables servings for children over the course of the day. Just start with fruit or carrot sticks for lunch, fruit for after school snacks and vegetables and a healthy protein source for dinner. The Australian Government and Nutrition Australia ran a public campaign in 2008[13] with the tag line – "Swap it, don't stop it" to encourage adults to swap less healthy options for healthier strategies. It's a great idea to teach children this concept as well and offers a great way of explaining a strategy for change to children.

R – Rest: De-stress

Rest and sleep are extremely important for children and adults to be able to focus, concentrate and self-regulate their emotions. I'm sure you can relate that when your child doesn't sleep, you don't either. Then the next day is extremely hard for all as you try and get through what you need to do.

Why is this?

At a neurobiological level, emotion regulation involves the interaction of subcortical brain structures of the limbic system (our Limbo) that generate emotional responses to stimuli with control centres – the prefrontal cortex (our Leader) that regulate emotional responses and behaviour[14]. Given that the brain structures and neurochemicals involved in the regulation of emotion also govern sleep[15], and nearly all affective disorders co-occur with sleep abnormalities[16][17], an intimate relationship between these two domains of functioning is intuitive.[18]

What does this really mean. Basically, the chemicals that impact self regulation (being able to maintain a 'just right' level of alertness and being in control of our emotions) also are linked to good sleep habits. If our children don't get good sleep, or are waking during the night and not resettling, then emotional regulation during the day is going to be impacted.

Children need more sleep than adults to best be able to learn, function and control their emotions. So how much sleep should we be encouraging?

- Babies should aim for 14-15 hours per day, split between night time sleep and naps.
- 1-3- year-olds need 12-14 hours per day and in this stage, they normally drop from two to one nap during the day
- 3-6-year-olds need 10-12 hours per day, and tend to drop their day time nap between 3-4 years old

- 7-12-year-olds need 10-11 hours per day. At this stage, bedtimes gradually get later, with most 12-year-olds going to bed about 9 p.m.
- 12-18-year-olds need 8-9 hours per day. However, with study and social pressure and the temptations of increased screen time use at night, their sleep can be greatly compromised, resulting in sleep deprivation. Teenagers may actually need more sleep than when they were younger as their brain grows and adjusts to the teenage brain growth.[19]

The Link between Sleep Difficulties and Anxiety in Children

Candace Alfano, principal investigator of a research project and the director of the Sleep and Anxiety Centre of Houston, believes children who experience inadequate or disrupted sleep are more likely to develop depression and anxiety disorders later in life.[20] Alfano reports that "healthy sleep is critical for children's psychological well-being and continually experiencing inadequate sleep can eventually lead to depression, anxiety and other types of emotional problems. Parents, therefore, need to think about sleep as an essential component of overall health in the same way they do nutrition, dental hygiene and physical activity. If your child has problems waking up in the morning or is sleepy during the day, then their night time sleep is probably inadequate. This can result for several reasons, such as a bedtime that is too late, non-restful sleep during the night or an inconsistent sleep schedule."[21]

Deb's Top 7 Ideas for Encouraging Good Sleep

1. Create a good routine and stick to a sleep schedule

Create a visual program of the night routine (make a list of what comes first, then next) and then get your child to help you illustrate it or choose clipart to decorate it with a picture. Laminate and cut it out and put it on a clip board or another laminated sheet with each task in the right order and the times next to the task. Stick it on with Blu Tack or Velcro so you can move it around as needed. Try and keep a similar time and routine but understand that life happens, and things may change. By using the visuals, your anxious child will be able to check whenever they want.

A sample visual might look something like this:

6 p.m. – Dinner
6.30 p.m. – Bath
7 p.m. – Stories in bed
7.20 p.m. – Quiet reading in Bed
7.40 p.m.– Lights out

Try and keep similar wake and sleep times throughout the weekend, too, to keep the routine going.

2. Get the light right

This can have a massive impact on children's sleep – wake cycles. Encourage children to be outside in the morning light, soaking up the lovely blue light, and encourage time outside during the day.

Conversely, at night we need to avoid blue light, which stimulates the brain and makes it more alert. This means avoiding all screens for at least 2 hours before bedtime.

Many children I work with, and many parents I know, give their child screen time late in the day and just before bedtime to help them "relax". However, research has shown that blue light increases alertness and is not helpful for getting to sleep, especially interactive blue light activities, such as interactive games. The blue light emitted from screens actually delays the release of sleep-inducing melatonin, increases alertness, and resets the body's internal clock (circadian rhythm) to a later schedule. It not only takes children longer to get to sleep, but it also decreases REM sleep (when we dream and process important learning into our long term memories) and children can wake up sleepier, even when they get the correct amount of sleep.[22]

In our typical sleep-wake cycle, melatonin levels tend to rise two hours prior to sleep onset.[23] This is why research recommends limiting exposure to screens 1-2 hours prior to bed time.[24][25]

3. Avoid late meals or drinks

A large meal can cause indigestion that interferes with sleep and drinking too late will increase the times a child needs to wake up to go to the toilet or cause wet beds which mean that both the child and you as the parent may be up during the night.

4. Avoid naps after 3pm

For children who still nap, or come home from school tired, napping after 3 p.m. can make it very difficult to get back to sleep. Keep them busy, serve an early dinner and get them to bed earlier if they need it.

5. Avoid activities that keep them up

This might include playing games, cruising the internet or being on social media (with the additional difficulty of the blue light (as discussed above). It might also be other activities such as night sports or trying to get homework or projects done. Encourage your child to develop good time management skills early in life. Map out when homework and projects are due and encourage them to do a little each night and perhaps more on the weekends to avoid those last-minute project efforts.

6. Encourage a relaxing night time routine and environment

Having a regular and calming night time routine and environment creates a safe place for your anxious child. When they feel calmer, their Limbo is relaxed, they are happier and will be able to feel safe and secure for settling into a bedtime and pre-sleep routine.

Here are some more ideas that work well for many children:

- Include a bath or shower to help your child relax
- Burn some essential oils, dim the lights or use lamps to create a calmer and darker environment
- String up LED fairy lights in your child's room, and
- Create a cosy tent structure over your child's bed or buy a pre-made tent structure. There are a few different ideas on the market including a pop-up tent that fully encloses the bed and is cosy like a camping tent, or bed canopies.

7. Take a hot bath before bed

After a bath your body temperature drops, which may help your child feel sleepy and the bath will also help them relax.[26]

S – Serve

66 If you want happiness for an hour, take a nap. If you want happiness for a day, go fishing. If you want happiness for a year, inherit a fortune. If you want happiness for a lifetime, help somebody. 99

Chinese Proverb

Modelling and teaching children to serve is a fantastic goal to work towards and a great way to develop empathy and resilience in children. A resilient child is more self-confident, feels competent in their skills, is connected to people around them, feels that they are contributors to their family, school and communities and feel more in control of their life and their emotions, including levels of stress and anxiety.

With the right service opportunities from kindergarten through high school, young people can grow from an understanding of how they fit into society to how they can help solve societal problems. This developmental process grows empathy and fosters children's identities as engaged citizens.[27]

Service can also be a strategy for the anxious child to feel connected, fit in and "pass the time" during parts of the routine which may produce anxiety. One of my sons finds it awkward and hard to know what to do before school and during the long lunch time. Yes, he loves playing handball and being social some days, but not all the time. He needs some introvert time to pull away from the noise of the playground. So, he has connected with his kitchen teacher and volunteers before school and during some lunchtimes to help clean the kitchen, prepare and organise food for the next classes and help out however he can. He's not the only one either. There's a little group of students who love to help out. It helps reduce the anxiety of being on the playground and gives them a sense of purpose. Children who suffer from stress and anxiety often find it really helpful to know the routine of day as they know what to expect and what's coming up.

66 Recess and lunch times can be really stressful and anxiety-producing as it's often a time for free play, which our anxious kids find hard to cope with. 99

In addition, lunch time also poses many sensory challenges, such as noise from children playing and bright light from being outside, which can exacerbate feelings of being out of control and produce anxiety.

Providing opportunities both at home and in the school program to encourage children to think about and help others rather than themselves and their own gain is a great way to help children develop resiliency. There's some great research to show that one of the things that predicts whether or not children will be more hopeful and optimistic as they grow and develop is if you provide opportunities where they could help others, you do charitable activities as a family, starting at an early age.[28]

We all like to be thanked for contributing to our world, and when children hear "thank you" for their contributions both at home and outside the family, they will be encouraged to contribute more to the world around them. This is why it's so important to teach children the importance of helping others and encourage a 'can do' approach.[29]

There are many volunteer programs that encourage young people to connect and give back to their communities. These include Rotary Youth Programs[30], StormCo (Service to Others Really Matters Company),[31] or UNyouth[32], to name a few. There are many service opportunities for families with children of different ages, as well as teenagers and young adults.

For teaching kindness in the classroom, or to get ideas for your children at home, the Random Acts of Kindness website[33] has some great ideas for inspiring you on how to start. They have free Kindergarten to Year 8 lesson plans that you could also use as ideas for sharing with your child at home.

Be inspired! You don't have to join an organisation or travel to a developing country to volunteer (although this is fun and very rewarding and could be a long-term family project). Start by encouraging your anxious child to reach out to others they see every day and see them develop confidence and connectedness (and reduced stress and anxiety)!

---

[1] D Morton (2018) *Live More Happy*. Signs Publishing.

[2] Smith, K. A. & Gouze, K. R. (2004). *The Sensory-Sensitive Child: Practical Solutions for Out-of-bounds Behaviour*. Harper Collins.

[3] Ledoux, J. (1998). *The Emotional Brain: The Mysterious Underpinnings of Emotional Life*. Simon and Schuster.

[4] Coren, S., Porac,C., & Ward, L.M. (1984). *Sensation and Perception*. Harcourt Brach Jovanovich.

[5] https://www.salford.ac.uk/cleverclassrooms/1503-Salford-Uni-Report-DIGITAL.pdf

[6] Lam, et al, op cit; J S Terman, M Terman, E Lo and T B Cooper (2001) *Circadian time morning light administration and therapeutic response in winter depression*. Archives of General Psychiatry, 58, pp 69-75.

[7] https://sosapproach-conferences.com/

[8] M Pollan (2008), In Defense of Food, Penguin Press, in D Morton (2018) *Live More Happy*. Signs Publishing.

[9] Beezhold, B. L., Johnston, C. S., and Daigle, D. R. (2010). *Vegetarian diets are associated with healthy mood states: A cross-sectional study in Seventh Day Adventist adult*. Nutrition Journal, 9, page 26.

[10] Lai, J. S.,Hiles, S.,Bisquera, A., Hure, A. J., McEvoy, M., and Attia, J. (2014). *A systematic review and meta-analysis of dietary patterns and depression in community-dwelling adults*. American Journal of Clinical Nutrition, 99(1), pages 181-97.

[11] McMartin, S.E., Jacka, F. N., and Colman, I. (2013). *The association between fruit and vegetable consumption and mental health disorders: Evidence from five waves of a national survey of Canadians.* Preventive Medicine, 56, pages 225-30.

[12] Payne, M. E., Steck, S. E., George, R. R. and Steffens, D. C. (2012). *Fruit, Vegetable and Antioxidant Intakes are Lower in Older Adults with Depression.* Journal of the Academy of Nutrition and Dietetics, 112(12), pages 2022-7.

[13] http://www.nutritionaustralia.org/act/swap-it-dont-stop-it-workplace-services

[14] Ochsner KN, Gross JJ. *The neural bases of emotion and emotion regulation: a valuation perspective,* In: Gross JJ, editor, Handbook of emotion regulation. End ed. New York: Guilford: 2014, p. 23-42

[15] Goldstein AN, Ealker MP. *The role of sleep in emotional Brain function.* Anna Rev Clin Psuchol 2014; 10:679-708.

[16] Alfano CA, Gamble AL. *The role of sleep in childhood psychiatric disorders.* Youth Care Forum 2009;38:327 – 40.

[17] Harvey, AG. *Sleep and circadian functioning: critical mechanisms in the mood disorders?* Anna Rev Clin Psuchol 2011; 7:297-319.

[18] https://www.researchgate.net/publication/290648938_Sleep_and_Emotion_Regulation_An_Organizing_Integrative_Review#pf9

[19] https://www.webmd.com/parenting/guide/sleep-children#1

[20] Cara A. Palmer, Candice A. Alfano. *Sleep and emotion regulation: An organizing, integrative review.* Sleep Medicine Reviews, 2016

[21] https://www.sciencedaily.com/releases/2016/07/160722104137.htm

[22] https://sleepfoundation.org/sleep-topics/how-blue-light-affects-kids-sleep

[23] Zawilska JB, Skene DJ, Arendt J. *Physiology and pharmacology of melatonin in relation to biological rhythms.* Pharmacol Rep 2009;61:383–410.

[24] American Academy of Paediatrics Policy Statement: Children, adolescents, and the media. *Paediatrics* 2013;132:958–61.

[25] Sleep Health Foundation. *Ten tips for a good night's sleep. Sydney: Sleep Health Foundation,* 2014. Available at www.sleephealthfoundation.org.au/fact-sheets-az/225-tips-for-a-good-night-sleep.html [Accessed 27 July 2015]

[26] https://www.nhlbi.nih.gov/files/docs/public/sleep/healthysleepfs.pdf

[27] https://www.psychologytoday.com/us/blog/the-moment-youth/201506/grow-childs-empathy-in-3-easy-ways

[28] https://www.kidsinthehouse.com/all-parents/parenting/resilience/developing-resilience-helping-others

[29] https://exploreanddevelop.com.au/raising-resilient-children/

[30] http://rotaryaustralia.org.au/youth-programs

[31] https://stormco.adventistconnect.org/about-us

[32] https://unyouth.org.au/

[33] https://www.randomactsofkindness.org/

A. Breathing Strategies

Breathing is an automatic process, but to some extent we can control it. By becoming aware of how we are breathing and by altering it if necessary, we can reduce body stress and improve recovery time from meltdowns or tantrums. The key to this is learning 'deep breathing'. Children's yoga or Pilates, for example, and various forms of sustained exercise and stretching can teach the value and significance of drawing air deep into the lungs and exhaling completely in a slow, controlled manner – a simple process that generates a sense of calm and control.

Teaching children to utilise proper 'deep' breathing techniques can help them deal with situations they might otherwise find overwhelming, such as test-anxiety, visits to doctors or dentists, or new social situations.

There are a few simple techniques you can teach a child to help them get started with relaxation, or 'deep' breathing.

- Talk to the child about what relaxation or deep breathing is, how it is different from regular breathing, and when it is a good idea to use it. You can begin by explaining that calm breathing is meant to be a lot slower than normal breathing, and that it's a great tool to use when they become stressed or upset. For example, if a child is anxious about lining up to pick up their lunch from the canteen or cafeteria at school, tell them to try deep breathing while they are waiting in line. Understand that children will probably have questions and will be unsure how to do what you are suggesting. Practising breathing strategies while they are calm and not worried (when the Leader is in charge and the Limbo is calm) is very important so they can draw on these new skills when they are stressed and worried.

- Allow time for children to settle and get their wiggles out before the relaxation practice starts. Create a comfortable, soothing environment and use comfortable floor mats and calming music, if available. Help them relax by dimming lights, closing blinds, talking softly or using a story or relaxation script to help them relax and settle.

- When practising, sit across from the child, making sure that you have their undivided attention. Explain to them in detail how you are going to take a deep breath, and that you want them to watch closely and copy you when they are ready. Let the child know that they may feel silly or weird at first, but as they practise, they will be able to do relaxation breathing anywhere at any time and chances are, no one will even notice.

- Place your hands on your stomach and take a deep breath in through your nose and hold it for just a few seconds before letting it out through your mouth. Demonstrate how the breathing is slower and how it can be felt in the stomach area. Repeat this several times until the child is ready to copy you. Let the child know that it's fine to repeat this breath as many times as they need to in order to feel better. To lighten up the mood of the breathing lesson, try incorporating some imaginary visuals. Have the child pretend to be blowing up a balloon or have them actually blow bubbles and let them notice how the deep breath in and slow release mimics what you have just shown them. This is an especially useful tool for younger children who can then recall that visual when they need to practise relaxation breathing.

- Once they are comfortable with the feeling of deep breathing the next step is to practise holding their breath for 10 seconds and then exhaling slowly, and then breathing in again. Repeating this for 10 breaths in and out will help to interrupt the body's physical response to stress.

B. Muscle Strategies

There are 3 main ways we can use our muscles to reduce feelings of stress. Each way is beneficial and calming to the nervous system.

1. Progressive muscle relaxation

One of the most valuable techniques to help children relax is progressive muscle relaxation. In the process of learning how to isolate and relax different muscle groups throughout their bodies, they are also practising the valuable art of mindfulness, of scanning and being aware of stress or tension in their muscles and learning to let go of it. As they become more familiar with the technique, they will be able to perform the exercise in any environment. With progressive muscle relaxation, the child is taken on a journey through their body, usually with the help of guided visual relaxation scripts. The focus is on noticing and relaxing muscles, especially those that tend to hold the most tension. A script is a written guide which the adult reads or speaks in a slow and calm voice, stepping the child through imagery and relaxation exercises.

The first step is to have the child focus on breathing, taking slow breaths in and out. (See the previous section for tips on using breathing for relaxation). Next, the child starts with an area of the body, usually the feet, and squeezes them or tenses the muscles. Then the child is instructed to let the tension go, to pay attention to how the release feels and to focus on keeping the muscles loose and light. For some children, releasing the muscles with a breath is most effective. The child then continues up through the body, focusing on the legs, torso, hands, arms, shoulders, neck, jaw and eyes. The goal is that once the exercise is finished, the child will feel more centred and relaxed with less tension in their body.

Keep practising these exercises with the child until they are able to progress through them at a faster pace while still achieving the desired effect. Always take the time to breathe with them and offer praise and encouragement for all their efforts.

When you start the process of teaching your child these techniques, you may find that they are one of the many children who struggle with being calm or 'slow' enough to lie down quietly and even begin to attempt a relaxation script or guided imagery exercise. If your child is going 'too fast' (refer to the *Just Right Kids*® diagram in chapter 1), try doing some resistance or 'muscle' activities. These might include arm wrestles, animal or crab walks, or floor or wall push ups. Next, move onto more passive 'muscle' games or activities such as stretches or yoga poses.

Follow these with some deep touch pressure activities (see below) such as a massage, or rolling and pressing firmly on the child's back, arms and legs with a fitness ball while the child is lying on their stomach (never roll a child's stomach when they are lying face upwards).

2. Stretching, yoga, Pilates and sustained muscle use

The second way of using our muscles is by stretching them for a longer time, for example, by holding yoga or Pilates poses for 10-30 seconds as opposed to a quick 'tense and relax'. There are many child-focused yoga and Pilates resources that can make these stretches fun.

As well as encouraging relaxation and relieving stress, yoga and Pilates help children:

- Increase self-confidence and self-esteem
- Improve concentration
- Focus more successfully
- Improve mental and physical health
- Increase awareness of themselves and their surroundings
- Remain calm during stressful situations.

Giving children an opportunity to engage in multiple types and levels of physical and mental activity is important to their growth and development and integrating stretching into their curriculum gives early access to a lifetime practice with ongoing benefits.

3. Active muscle use

The third way of using our muscles is by playing sports, playing on playground equipment, resistance in rough and tumble play, or riding a bike. Active or aerobic activity uses the muscles, delivers higher amounts of oxygen to the muscles, and increases blood flow. It releases endorphins and gives a sense of well-being.

Exercise and active muscle work are very important in reducing stress levels in both the short and the longer term, for children and adults.

C. Deep Touch Pressure

Therapy using the application of weight, or deep touch pressure therapy, is a sensory processing strategy which produces a sense of calm and relaxation. Weighted blankets, weighted lap packs and pressure vests are designed to deliver pressure at specific points on the body. Children using deep touch therapy strategies often show a marked increase in their ability to relax, stay calm, concentrate, focus, learn, and become more engaged in learning.

These tools have been useful for children with ADHD, autism and other disorders involving hyperactivity, but they are also extremely useful for children with minor issues related to stress and overstimulation. There is a wide range of products available and they can be used unobtrusively in a variety of settings to calm and relax. Research and experience have shown that as little as 5-10% of the subject's body weight is enough to produce a beneficial calming effect in both children and adults.

You can try out these products on your own, but the best results are achieved under the guidance of a trained therapist with experience in sensory processing. Weighted blankets especially should only be used be used under supervision to help with calming and settling and they should never be left on overnight.

CHAPTER 11

Cognitive and thinking strategies to reduce stress (top down approaches)

A. Visualisation Strategies

Guided visualisation offers one of the most effective ways of teaching a child how to remove themselves from a stressful situation long enough to become centred and approach a problem with a fresh perspective and a renewed sense of calmness. Guided visualisation scripts for children are specially created to appeal to the imagination and sensory exploration of the young mind.

Before using a guided visualisation with a child, bring them into a quiet, comfortable place. Make sure their body is comfortable. If they are fidgety, try having them sit or lie in a bean bag; this might calm them by providing some deep touch pressure. Or give them a 'hand fidget' – for example, a squishy ball or a soft piece of material to fiddle with. Some children may prefer sitting in a soft comfortable chair or lying on the floor amid cushions.

Use slow, methodical speech when going through the visualisation and check constantly to see whether your child is following. Look for signs that they are relaxing, breathing slower, and looking more chilled and relaxed. The goal of these exercises is to teach the child how to focus on listening to instructions and being able to imagine going to a new and relaxing place.

We have included two sample visualisation scripts to assist you in practising guided visualisation with your child.

"Wow! I'm going to try this
with my son and my clients.
I love it! It's so indepth!"

Peta, Mum and Mental Health Worker

Guided Visualisation Number One: Butterflies in the Mirror

Progressive Relaxation Using Guided Visualisation

We are going to sit and spend some time imagining. We are doing this to help you relax. If you feel uncomfortable at any time, you are free to tell me you want to stop. We are doing this so that you feel happy.

First, I want you to sit back or lie down and close your eyes. I want you to visualise, or see in your mind, or think about, your body. Pretend that you are looking in a mirror and can see yourself.

With your eyes still closed, imagine you are looking at yourself in the mirror and notice your feet. Look how firmly they are placed on the ground and feel how strong they are. Now you can pretend to be barefoot or wearing shoes, it is up to you. Wiggle your toes a little and then let them relax. Take a deep breath as you feel your feet touching the ground. Imagine breathing in your favourite colour and watch it travel all the way to your toes.

Next, see your legs in the mirror. Think of all the fun things they help you do. Think for a moment about how they feel when you are running and playing. Tighten your leg muscles up just a little, like you do when you are about to jump. But instead of jumping imagine yourself holding still with your tightened muscles for just a minute. Take a deep breath in and then breathe out, releasing your strong leg muscles and letting them relax.

Now your toes and your legs are relaxed.

When you imagine yourself in the mirror, you start to smile as your body becomes more relaxed.

We are going to continue moving up through your body now.

Sit tall in the chair (or relax more if you are lying down) and imagine your stomach. Have you ever been so excited or happy about something that you were able to feel it in your stomach? Some people call that feeling butterflies. Imagine beautiful, colourful butterflies fluttering around your stomach. You can just barely feel them tickling your skin as they flutter about. The tickling makes you tighten your stomach muscles just a little, just like you do when you are laughing. Take a deep breath in, hold it for a moment and then let it go. Imagine the butterflies flying up toward the sky. They are happy and free as you breathe out the tightness in your stomach.

You are starting to really feel relaxed now.

Imagine looking at yourself in the mirror again. You are surrounded by your favourite colour and brilliant butterflies playfully float above you.

Next, let your arms fall to your side. Don't try to hold them up, just let them hang there. Can you feel your fingers stretching towards the ground? Let them stretch as much as they want. Think of yourself as a tree; your arms are the branches that are reaching down to touch the Earth.

You are happy and strong. There is nothing that can harm you and you have nothing to worry about.

Pretend again that you are looking at yourself in the mirror. This time imagine looking at your face. Think about your jaw and your teeth. If they are feeling tight, just let them relax. Picture your mouth making a smile instead of a frown. Visualise in your mind how much better it feels when you smile.

Finally, it is time to think about your eyes. Picture what colour they are and think about something happy that they helped you see today. Your eyes are wonderful and they help you see all the beautiful things in the world. Stay quiet and still for just a moment while thinking about something happy that you have seen. Take slow deep breaths while you are thinking.

Imagine yourself in the mirror one more time. You and your body are completely relaxed and happy. Anything that was making you upset or sad is all gone. You are surrounded by beauty and happiness.

Now, open your eyes and tightly wrap your arms around yourself. Give yourself a big squeeze. Your body is now strong, calm and relaxed. Take one more deep breath in and then slowly let it out. Now stand up.

Guided Visualization Number Two: The Magical Waterfall

To begin, I want you to sit where you are comfortable. Try to find a comfortable position that allows your feet to touch the ground.

Now that you are comfortable, close your eyes and slowly take a deep breath in through your nose. Now let it out just as slowly through your mouth. Feel your breath pass over your lips.

If you are comfortable with it, I want you to keep your eyes closed while I talk. I am going to take you on a journey with my words and while I am doing that I want you to use your imagination to create pictures in your mind. If you can, try to imagine yourself in these pictures. You are free to do anything you want in your imagination. You can run, play and stop to touch and smell anything you want along the way.

With your eyes closed, imagine that you are standing barefoot in the sand. The sand feels warm around your toes. You can wiggle your toes and feel them sink into the warm sand. You look around and you are at a beach. The sun is warm and you can feel it on your face and hands. You can hear seagulls, and the voices of other children playing in the distance. It is a beautiful day.

Imagine looking over to water. There are soft waves that crawl up to the sand. You decide to walk over to the water. Imagine the feeling of the sand beneath your feet with each step and think about how the sand changes the closer you get to the water. It goes from very warm to almost cool as the sand becomes thicker and a little muddy from the water splashing onto it. Your feet are cool and happy as you stand on the beach near the water.

Take a deep breath in and think about your favourite thing to do at the beach. Maybe you want to go swimming in the cool water or sit down and start building a sandcastle. You can do whatever makes you happy. Just for a minute, think about how the water or sand feels on the rest of your body - on your knees or your hands. Feel your entire body being happy and relaxed while you enjoy your special beach day.

Look up into the sky. It is the prettiest blue you have ever seen and off in the distance you can see a rainbow behind a big, fluffy white cloud. Everything around you is perfect. While you are playing, you hear a gurgle. You decide to wander off and investigate the noise. In a corner of the beach which you hadn't seen before, you notice a small magical waterfall. At the bottom of the waterfall are sparkling rocks, all smooth and beautiful. You sit down at the edge of the waterfall and touch one of the rocks with your hand. You carefully pick it up and feel how smooth it is.

When you reach down to touch the rock you notice how cool and refreshing the water is. You take just a little bit of water in your hand and pour it over your face, letting it trickle slowly down your nose and lips. It tickles a bit. Imagine how cool it feels and how happy you are to be playing in the magical water.

Even though there are other kids around playing at the beach, you know that this magical spot is just for you. You are the only one that can touch the sparkling rocks and play in the magical water. This is your special place and you only have to share if you want to. This is the place that you can come to when you want to feel happy and magical.

You decide to stand up and return to the beach, knowing that your waterfall will always be there for you and that you can always stay as long as you want. You bend down and pick up one small rock to take with you. You will keep this rock in your pocket as a reminder of this special place.

As you are walking back to beach, imagine yourself standing in the same place that you started, with the warm sand around your toes and the sun shining down on you. Take a deep breath and slowly open your eyes.

When you are feeling anxious or sad, you can always close your eyes and return to this place on your own. The next time you are outside, pick out a smooth rock that seems magical to you. Keep it in your pocket and rub it with your fingers when you are worried or upset. This rock will help remind you of your special waterfall.

Children love to know what's coming up. They love to anticipate events, and by knowing what is planned for the day and for the week they are able to feel safer.

Giving notice to children when their routine is going to change is really important for all children. This can include telling children that their after-school activity has been cancelled for that day or that their childcare arrangements have had to be changed.

When transitions such as going back to school are upcoming or in progress, children may feel anxious or worried. Their daily and weekly routine is changing, which can be unsettling. Signs of mild to moderate anxiety might look like a child struggling to get out of bed, more complaining or whining than usual, complaints of feeling sick, or being on the toilet excessively. More severe signs of anxiety might include the above but might also include tears, anger or other 'behavioural' outbursts.

Supporting children during these times of change can reduce their anxiety and stress considerably. One way of doing this is to create a routine board for the week. Involving your child in its creation and decoration helps to increase their feeling of ownership and an increased sense of control over their routine. Print off a blank calendar from the Internet, print off some pictures or clipart and find pictures in magazines. Add in pictures for the regular routine activities such as breakfast, teeth brushing and getting ready etc.

Once you have a visual routine, you can ask your child to check where they are up to every day, rather than having to remind them to do the next thing. Encourage your child to 'tick off' each task as they go, or take it off the chart and put it into a 'finished' box.

For after school activities, add in activities such as swimming or dance lessons or after school care days. Don't over commit your children. Kids need down time, free time and even 'boring' time every week. These free time activities should be screen-free and help children to learn how to be imaginative, come up with new ideas for play, read a book, or sit and listen to music. Free and unstructured time is rare for both children and adults but is very precious and extremely important for children's development.

When you are planning your child's routine, remember to allow time for active play, like playing at the park, team sports, jumping on the trampoline. Each of these are important in different ways to develop coordination, social and other core developmental skills. But it's important for children to have active time to develop healthy routines, not only for keeping fit and healthy as adults, but also for valuing physical activity as a child and adult in reducing stress and improving mental health.

When we help our child to plan out their week and know and understand what is coming up, we are empowering their Leader (frontal cortex) to truly be the leader and to take charge of the Limbic system, to have greater control over their emotions. They feel more independent as they can check for themselves (by looking on their daily or weekly planning board) about what is coming up if they start to feel worried or unsure. The goal of parenting is to encourage age-appropriate independence and by developing strategies to reduce anxiety, we can help our children engage in and do what they need to do.

Conclusion

Stress is a normal part of everyday life. We need a certain level of it to get things done, and as adults, we have generally developed the skills to cope with stress through a lifetime of experience. But children have a lot to learn and are not yet adept at dealing with stressful or anxiety producing situations. While some children cope just fine, others are more sensitive. There may even be specific triggers that cause a child to go into a state of anxiety. Understanding the kinds of issues that children face on a daily basis, at home and at school, and understanding why these issues put pressure on your child is the key to helping them deal with and overcome stress.

There are many reasons why a child may feel anxiety and exhibit symptoms of stress. It could be fear, peer conflicts or bullying, sibling rivalry, academic pressures, changes to routine, or sensory overload. Any of these factors can cause a child to become non-responsive, withdraw, complain and whine more than usual, or exhibit disruptive behaviours. Children of all ages need some level of stability to feel safe and secure.

It is important to teach our children how to recognise stressful situations, label the emotions they are feeling, and introduce them to effective strategies for dealing with such situations. Learning to manage challenging situations and self-regulation is essential to set them up for the future. And it all begins with support.

While helping a child with sensory overload or sensory processing issues can be complex, there are a few simple strategies you can implement which will help children cope. These might include:

- Planning ahead for stressful situations (Top down approaches for empowering our Leader)
- Visualisation and breathing techniques (Mastering our Limbo)
- Limiting screen-time, including TV, computers, phones and tablets (Keep our Limbo under control)
- Encouraging outdoor play and activity (support the Limbo to be calm so that the Leader can lead)
- Creating sensory safe spaces within the home and the classroom (to keep a calm body), and
- Modelling acceptable behaviour and emotional reactions

An important way of helping children cope with stress is through the process of self-regulation. Teaching a child to recognise and understand their own emotions is the first step towards teaching emotional control and independence. The *Just Right Kids® Model* was developed for this very purpose. It uses analogies that even young children can easily understand and provides a tool for them to learn to identify and vocalise their feelings.

Different emotions trigger different responses, and these are often physical. For example, a child who is angry experiences stress reactions which might include tightness of shoulders, sweating, or clenching of fists. The child whose body is tired needs rest and recovery. The child whose body is Just Right has both their body and their emotions under control, and their sensory experiences appropriately processed. The *Just Right Kids® Model* teaches them to understand the physical signs of the emotion they are feeling.

Sections Two and Three of this book provide strategies and techniques for helping children cope with the stressors of daily life, from hints and tips on how to prepare, to guided visualisations to encourage 'bodily knowing' and relaxation. It is not necessary to put all of them in place, but do try them out and identify the ones that work for your own child. They may feel a little strange at first but learning to relax and calm the body is a huge part of self-regulation. And learning to self-regulate leads to emotional stability and control.

Use stressful or anxious times in a child's life as teachable moments. Give your child tools to recognise how they feel and tools to self regulate. Don't try and FIX the situation for them. TEACH and SUPPORT them......

It is my sincere hope that this book has been helpful for both you and your child in learning to communicate your feelings, identify stressful situations and take control of emotions, so that you can live a calmer and more empowered life together. Remember, everything is a learning experience, and we all have our own way of learning.

Deb

66 You can be a superhero for your family with these practical strategies! 99

www.ingramcontent.com/pod-product-compliance
Lightning Source LLC
Chambersburg PA
CBHW070645150426
42811CB00051B/755